Jonestown
a new look at
dimensions from a Guyanese perspective

Eusi Kwayana

Limited Edition

Los Angeles, California

Copyright & Related

Copyright
©2019 by Eusi Kwayana

ISBN
ISBN-13: 9781797071435

Publisher
Carib House
11305 Goleta St
Los Angeles (Sylmar), CA 91342-6524
Email: CaribHouse@Outlook.com
Web: CaribHouse.Org

Contact
Inquiries and Orders:
Eusi Kwayana

68 Eastwyck Road, Decatur, GA 30032

Email: eusirurakwa@gmail.com

Country of Origin
Printed & Bound in the USA

All Rights Reserved
Except for fair use reproduction and application, prior written permission is required from the author in all other cases.

Credits

Rosaliene Bacchus—Proofreading.

Ashton Franklin—Cover design and cover art.

Laura Johnston Kohl—Reading and editing the manuscripts. As a Peoples Temple member who served both in Guyana and California, Laura brought an eye witness experience of Jonestown to bear on the book. As a successful author herself, she continues to have an abiding interest in all things Jonestown and devotes her life to perpetuate its memory.

Fielding McGehee—Reading and editing the manuscripts. As principal researcher at the Jonestown Institute (SDSU), Professor McGehee was a knowledgeable resource on Temple's history and offered invaluable guidance and advice. He is the editor of *the jonestown report*, which is an on-line and printed digest of articles about Peoples Temple written by survivors and Jonestown scholars.

Rebecca Moore—Reading and editing the manuscripts. Rebecca is the author of a number of scholarly books and articles about Peoples Temple. Apart from a scholar and educator, Professor Moore is a family member of several Jonestown victims. She has personal insights on the subject and readily shared her unique perspective.

P. D. Sharma—Interior design, layout and format.

Acknowledgement

Mr. Kwayana wishes to thank the patrons named below who prepuchased significant multiple copies. The proceeds therefrom as well as from individual copies taken by other well-wishers — all before publication — enabled the eventual printing of this book. Heartfelt thanks to all of you.

Bathersfield, Arnold (Cheverly, MD, USA)

Easton, Keith (Lanham, MD, USA)

Hergash, Harry (Toronto, Canada)

Huntley, Eric (London, England)\

Kanhai, Rohit (Valley Stream, NY 11580)

Karran, Bayney (Bethesda, MD, USA)

London, Remington & Berneta (Mansfield, NJ, USA)

Massay, John (Arverne, NY, USA)

Matsimela, Baba Mosi (Burtonsville, MD, USA)

Ram, Christopher (Georgetown, Guyana)

Seecharran, Clem (Warwickshire, England)

Stephenson, Aubrey (NW Washington, DC, USA)

Forthcoming Book

"ATTENTION GRABBING... HIGHLY ENTERTAINING CONVERSATION, FULL OF HISTORICAL FACTS." —*Dr. Juliet Emanuel*

EUSI KWAYANA

THINKER, SCHOLAR, TEACHER, LEADER

WITH DAVID HINDS

An Interview

THE LEGEND

POST-EMANCIPATION VILLAGES IN GUYANA: MAKING WORLD HISTORY

Foreword

Mr. Eusi Kwayana has been a good friend for the past ten years. We have had many discussions about Peoples Temple and Guyana, a subject we are both passionate about. I often try to sit around Eusi Kwayana at Peoples Temple survivor gatherings. His wise understanding of the Guyanese perspective always expands my own thinking.

When Eusi spoke about writing a book, I was elated. At this point, there are seven books written by survivors. Tim Reiterman (who was part of Congressman Ryan's group, and who was shot at the airstrip but survived) co-wrote *Raven*, Hyacinth Thrash wrote *The Onliest One Alive*, Deborah Layton wrote *Seductive Poison*, Leslie Wagner-Wilson wrote *Slavery of Faith*, Terri Buford wrote a book of Jonestown-inspired poetry *Jonestown Lullaby: Poems and Pictures*, Kathy Tropp Barbour published a wonderful book of photos of the Jonestown victims called *Who Died*, and I wrote my book *Jonestown Survivor: An Insider's Look*. I am only including people who had first-hand knowledge of Peoples Temple. When I first returned from being part of Peoples Temple for nine years, with the last two in Jonestown and Georgetown, Guyana, I had a very limited view of the horrific tragedy. I thought about a small group of survivors who were with me at the end. I couldn't take in that there was a much larger community that was devastated as well. I couldn't see much of anything through my pain. That was thirty-seven years ago. I fought my own demons over these years. No survivor lives without guilt to this day.

I have a continually evolving perspective on all things Peoples Temple. My first ten years were all about survival. My next decade was about setting up a new life with my family, my profession, etc. The next mountain I climbed was to reconnect with my dearest friends who shared the tragedy with me. And then, write my book. I published it in 2010.

Over the past ten years, since meeting and getting to know Eusi, and being in contact with more people from the international community, I had a new insight. I have finally realized that Jonestown was not only a personal disaster, a disaster for other survivors, a tragedy for all family members and intimate friends of all of the Peoples Temple members, and people in communities impacted by the deaths in Jonestown. The calamity of Jonestown deeply affected our country, without a doubt. But, it was disastrous for Guyana, for the government and for the people. The catastrophe of the deaths brought a new level of violence to this beautiful and diverse nation that has not recovered. The truth remains elusive in Guyana as well as everywhere else. And, that misfortune has been shared with the rest of the world as the ripples continue.

When I read the comprehensive and fascinating history of Peoples Temple from the Guyanese point of view, I was awestruck. Eusi included wise declarations from many of Guyana's finest and most astute scholars. In addition to his own valuable reflections, he really covered the whole subject matter by bringing in other wise Guyanese.

I was particularly impressed with the writings and speeches of Jan Carew, Walter Rodney and Keith Scott in the book. Mr. Kwayana included these fine historians because he wants the topic reviewed, discussed, dissected, and fundamentally understood. It is complex, and it is not only because of Jim Jones as we knew of him in Peoples Temple. It has to do with many other things – who made a way for us in Guyana and why, who covered for us and why, and who to this day does not expose all the mystery and the deceit of the time?

And, Eusi Kwayana also includes an even bigger picture. He includes what happens when a rich group (in this case and in many other cases with white leadership) moves into a poor country, and the immediate influence that group has on at least some members of the government of the poorer nation. Mr. Eusi Kwayana's book does address Peoples Temple and Guyana. But, I think the magic of his book makes a much bigger point by discovering and sharing the details of the Guyanese debacle.

Laura Johnston Kohl
Jonestown Survivor
Author, and Bilingual Educator

Contents

Copyright & Related ii
Credits iii
Acknowledgement iv
Forthcoming Book v
Foreword vi

I. Members & Survivors 1

Ch. 01 — Using Distant Places to Solve U.S. Internal Race Problems 2
Ch. 02 — Out of the Depths, a Dignity Movement ... 27

II. Residents & Visitors 34

Ch. 03 — As Seen by Bystanders 35
Ch. 04 — Report of the Agri-Audit Task Force 51
Ch. 05 — In the Shadow of the Temple 59
Ch. 06 — The Peoples Temple and the Guyana Government 66

III. Analysts & Critics 81

Ch. 07 — The Jonestown Plantation 82
Ch. 08 — Context for Leo Ryan's Involvement with Jonestown 96
Ch. 09 — Jonestown: A Caribbean/Guyanese Perspective 113
Ch. 10 — Jonestown Revisited 137

IV. Editor & Compiler 145

    Ch. 11 — A State within a State 146
    Ch. 12 — Placing Guyana on History's Map 155
    Ch. 13 — On Jeannie Mills' Book *Six Years*
               with God 164
    Ch. 14 — Father Divine and Rev. Jim Jones 177
    Ch. 15 — Domestic Efforts vs. Peoples Temple's 184
    Ch. 16 — A Search for Reasons 192
    Ch. 17 — Race and Gender in the Peoples Temple .. 204
    Ch. 18 — Jones's Revolutionary Praxis 214

V. Appendix & Miscellany 230

    References 231
    People 235
    Places 243
    Organizations 247
    Miscellaneous Terms 251
    Map of Guyana 253
    Other Works by Kwayana 254
    About the Author 258

List of Images

    Cover of Kwayana's Next Book v
    P. D. Sharma's Investigating Team 71
    Cover of *Groundings* ... (new edition) 115
    Walter Rodney 117
    Masthead of *DayClean* (newsletter) 147
    Christine Miller 210
    Map of Guyana 253
    Eusi Kwayana 258

x

I Members & Survivors ✓

II   Residents & Visitors

III   Analysts & Critics

IV   Editor & Compiler

V Appendix & Miscellany

Chapter 1

Using Distant Places to Solve U.S. Internal Race Problems

Interviews with Peoples Temple Members and Survivors

Eusi Kwayana

This section features the stories of three survivors of Jonestown: Hue Fortson, Neva Sly Hargrave, and Laura Johnston Kohl. All of them were members of Peoples Temple. They all thought that the Temple, with its operations outside of the USA, would solve their respective race problems as experienced in the USA. The problem of race for Hue Fortson, a black American male, is obvious. How could race be a problem for Neva Sly Hargrave and Laura Johnston Kohl, two white American women? It is a problem in that their friends, families, neighbors, and associates might cast a disapproving eye at their acceptance of other groups as just as equal and free. With the Temple's egalitarian ideals, such a utopian state would be possible, they all thought, leaving the race problem behind in mainland USA.

The Peace Mission of Father Divine, which preceded the Peoples Temple, is also examined in this section from the point of view of its operations in solving the race problem of America, this time in the USA itself.

The format for the interviews is to show my questions in bold and to indent the answers below them in regular type.

Hue Fortson's Story

Hue Fortson, a former aide of Jones, was a keen developer and has many perspectives on Jonestown that were hardly discussed by others. He remains a pastor in the Los Angeles area, where he "found the Lord again," as he said to one of his elders. Fortson was in San Francisco on November 18, 1978, but lost his wife Rhonda and his son Hue Ishi in the tragedy there. In the post-November 18, 1978, years he had once wandered into a California university, bumped into a psychology professor and started a series of well-received lectures in university classrooms. From his testimony readers learned how the Peoples Temple planned to turn Guyana's natural resources to good effect.

In this interview pastor Hue Fortson begins his narrative with the time when his wife Rhonda and son had left for Jonestown and he was still in San Francisco working on the Guyana project.

Hue, go ahead and tell us your story.

Jones left me in San Francisco while my wife Rhonda and my son went down to Guyana. She went down late in 1977 and I in March, 1978. But I was dispatched back to San Francisco in September 1978 to raise equipment for some development in Jonestown.

My work was to seek to acquire in the Los Angeles area equipment for a wood working factory in Jonestown and equipment for a fish-based industry and trade. I was able to procure for free some old tanks and old equipment; got all the working equipment as donations from businesses. They gave it to me willingly when I told them that I was going down South America and that we had a project to obtain rare species of tropical fish not in the current marketplace and that we planned to market them in the States.

And sure enough when I was down there we were in the jungle. At one time we went to a certain portion inside of the jungle where there was a stream. In that stream there were rare species of tropical fish. They were of the family called Lyre Tails, a very beautiful fish. And so I had some tanks set up there in Jonestown, even under the senior citizens' homes.

There were stores in the Bay Area and even in New York and everybody was so excited that we found some tropical fish that were not on the market. Everybody wanted thousands of fish to be shipped to New York. So I was trying to work out the logistics and that is what I was doing and we were only supposed to be there for two months. And at the end of the two months we were told to leave the jungle/stream site and go back to the Jonestown center.

Were you in charge of business in Jonestown?
Yes, so far as procuring and purchasing. Sometimes, but it would be after the initial buyers, if you will—up here in the U.S. side—would make contact and they would say pick this up, or you should check this person or give you a check and an address. You would bring it back here where we can crate it, here in the Bay Area, and ship it down to Jonestown. Or, send me a check to pick up something for the administration in San Francisco.

Dimensions from a Guyanese Perspective

This is before you went to Jonestown?
His (i.e., Jones's) thing was to make sure we kept things going and to make sure everybody was plucked into the vision of going to Guyana. He made it look like a type of situation in which you go over there, enjoy yourself for six months at the max, and then you come back here being refreshed and renewed. That's the way he put it to us in the beginning.

When did you join the Temple?
I came into it late '71, early '72. I went to Guyana in March of 1978, and came back to the U.S. in September of the same year.

Did the Temple people like one another? All the people I have met say that that is one thing they missed.
Yes. You were pretty much trained to talk, just be yourself, and don't let anyone put you down for lack of knowledge and skills. That's the way he taught all of us. Respect who you are and more so respect yourself as a child of God. That's how he put it at that time. That's one of the reasons he gained so much momentum and gained so many people. No matter who you were, if you were "bad" and different from everybody else, he would work with you long enough probably to find out what really was your problem, what really was your issue, and find a way to show you that he loves you and that he would take care of you. From that you would come and join the Temple, over and over again. That's how he tied people. There were some really broken down on the inside that felt they weren't worth living. He could take those same people and transform them into persons that really wanted to live again and have a purpose in their lives. He would bring you out of the doldrums. Many

Eusi Kwayana

people came to realize that firstly they need to repay him, so any thing he would ask them they would do it readily.

Was his love genuine, do you think?
I really do believe that in the beginning, say for the first three years, when he was starting in Redwood Valley and in the San Francisco area, he was genuine. I think he was sincere in what he was doing but I think what really happened was that the local companies, if you will, in the immediate area, if you will, really took to this guy because he had the knack of showing that he could have concern and compassion for people. He would always try to see people as much as he could, clothe them, you name it! We had got one of our suppliers (I think the name is Synanon) to accept donations on our behalf. We had it set up in the Bay Area and received the donations. Because of his actions in showing what we were doing as a group as opposed to what some of the churches in the very same neighborhood were doing—that won him a lot of respect from business people and they would readily offer their services to help out in any whatever way they could.

Do you get any of that help where you are now on your own?
Ha, ha! You know what? For the past five years, the first four months that I was in this, a two-mile square area in the same area, I took down phone numbers, addresses, pastors' names, wrote them a nice little letter, saying we were new in the community and we wanted to know that we would be a blessing to them if we could all get together and have a food/clothing giveaway for needy people in the neighborhood, whoever needed it. The first church rejected me. The other churches never did send back information. So what do you do? The consensus is that they feel you are

trying to take their members. I said to them something like this. "Well, if you would have taken the time to talk with me, I could easily let you know that I am on a mission trying to do something else. I am in the area of helping people, so if there is any good idea I can get from anybody, that's what I like."

Was Jones influential in politics?
Yeah, in Los Angeles and the Bay Area. I can remember on any given day walking in Los Angeles. I arrive at the DA's office—what's his name? Yes, Councilman David Callahan. I got into the building just to get up on stage, shake hands, and get a picture. And he did even more so in San Francisco. He had some people actually in place. He was able to manipulate and get anything he needed.

In Guyana Bishop Jones denied having public flogging in his church. But others have said yes. Any experience?
I was part of it at one time in the sense that when anyone was being "disciplined"—that's what they called it—we were monitoring, and if the order was for ten spanks, we had to see to it that ten spankings were given. And if I remember right, there was an occasion when somebody was being spanked and somebody had counted wrong and we all had the wrong count. Jones got so angry with us because he said, "You all are supposed to be leaders and you allow the count to slip by." He apologized to the lady (being flogged) and we had to stand in line, and I received two swats for allowing it to slip by. I have been a part of that. It reminded me because not so much being swatted but I would be counting and if you allowed the count to go wrong you were swatted. So it was like a two-edged sword.

The other Party in Guyana, the PPP, you mentioned an incident in your speech at the showing of the film at San Diego State University in July 2006. Can you explain?

Two months before I went down I received a call from overseas, from one of his administrators (i.e., from Jonestown). They instructed me to do research in the town and find five thousand T-shirts. They were to be red. I didn't know at that time. I bought them and paid for them. I didn't know at the time the destination where they were going, and, as it were, we came through the airport to Customs. The Customs personnel were so friendly with the Temple that once you were from the Temple they would say, "Come through, comrade," and they wouldn't even search your bag. That was already set in place and many times they would have parties at the house in Lamaha Gardens and invite some of the guys to come over and drink beer. They even slept with some of the women, the white women. They had a thing for white women. They thought that was gold. We had beautiful black women but they would never gravitate to them.

And the red T-shirts?

I remember when I got into Jonestown, they take all your belongings and then take you to the tent area. There they would take your wallet, all your bags when you get there for the first time. It was everything, everything, next to a strip search, but they didn't actually do that (i.e., a strip search). They take everything from you.

Security, I guess?

I guess so. They thanked me for bringing the bags in. They said it was a great favor. Jones wanted them (the red T-Shirts) to do something. They didn't go into details but later on I found out what it was. They were to use them as their support in their rally against Forbes Burnham, the prime minister of Guyana. That was in March. His thing was he always wanted to play the divide and conquer game. That's what he did with my wife and me. My wife and son went down in October '77 and he told me, "You will be going behind her but we still need you (in the USA) to help us in San Francisco". In San Francisco they were doing a lot of crating, buying a lot of equipment. Just before Christmas, 1977, they decided that I needed to be up there so I was up there with him (in San Francisco) and the thing was that when I did get to Jonestown, my wife was at Lamaha Gardens at our headquarters. And she would stay there for anything like three weeks to a month, working. Then he would send me and say you are one of the young black men that I can really trust and I will have to send you to Georgetown to do some work for a few weeks. What they considered work was that I would go around and purchase like five thousand pounds of shark meat because the Guyanese people wouldn't touch it because it is a scavenger, shark meat.

What about Archie Ijames? Did you know him? Ijames?

It is pronounced "*Imes.*" The "J" is silent. Yes I knew him quite well. We were in the Temple. We hung out a lot together, and even after the Temple was destroyed he and his wife they came back into my life. They came back to town. They bought them a home somewhere in Florida. They were doing some evangelizing, traveling. They found the Lord again and they used to go around and tell everybody and that's what they devoted the rest of their lives to. [Archie Ijames died May 30, 1993.]

Archie Ijames was a tower of strength, don't you think?

A very brave man. He was from the old school, but he was a certified carpenter and yet he had the wisdom and knowledge of any other man that went to a four- or five-year college. Very, very, brave man. No, he is not alive. He died several years ago. He was elderly when I first met him in the Temple, but he got much older. I remember how he shared something with me that was quite unique. He used to come to L.A. every two years at least and he would always seek me out to sit and talk. And he told this story.

He said, "You know, I was with Jim for years from Indiana to Redwood Valley from Redwood Valley to Frisco and from Frisco to L.A. and to Redwood Valley and back and I went down to that jungle and when I went down to that jungle I said 'Okay, well, all this is not what it is really made out to be.' He said Jones didn't think I knew it, but Jones was going to have me bumped off. He sent me to the jungle along with this other young man to do some work and the other young man, Teddy Bear, was actually supposed to wipe him (Ijames) away but he couldn't do it. So he came back. Jones was upset. So I suggest that to get his record straight that he was still in charge. Teddy Bear said that he wanted to come back to the States to take care of a couple things and tie some ends up and come back to Jonestown to stay forever. And Jones spoke out publicly in a public meeting. 'If you go back, I feel that something going to happen to you, so I don't want you to go. But if you want to go, you can go.'"

His real name is Chris Lewis, but we call him Teddy Bear, big, strong guy.

Was Teddy Bear White, or Black?
He was black. And sure enough, Teddy Bear was the just three weeks to a month in the States. And somewhere he went and, mind you he is from that area. Yet, still, whoever these people were, somebody began shooting guns at him and got into a gun battle. They had shot him once, and then, he went to a house and was banging on the door, trying to get some help, get the police, hoping they would let him in. They didn't let him in, but whoever these people were came up to him and emptied their guns. He had a thousand dollars in his pocket so it was not robbery. Then, after Jones got the news that Teddy Bear was dead, he made it the news of his story, his prophesy.

One writer said that although African Americans were a majority at Jonestown and had departmental responsibilities, they were not equally represented on the Planning Commission. What is your experience?
Well, I would put it this way. In the Planning Commission there were an equal number of blacks forever. But his top echelons, if that is a word I could use, that were around him that really made the real decisions were several white women, some that he had already compromised and slept with and they would do anything. And, mark you, he would have meetings with us after we already had an all-day meeting with him, the people, or congregation if you will. At 8.00 p.m. we were required to report to him whatever role that was assigned to us and many folks would bring coffee cups, pillow, and blankets because it was so cold, and other crazy thing would happened to come up on the agenda. It would end up being brought forth from the floor. You couldn't sleep because they would wake you up and it would always start off basically who slept with whom,

who didn't finish the assignment that was given to them at the last meeting

Postscript

To complete the Fortson story, I am adding the following comments.

Fortson did not report the harassing of Ijames on the voyage from Florida to Guyana on the Temple's boat. Tim Reiterman, co-author of the book *Raven* (Reiterman, 1982), who says that Ijames cooperated with him, explained it in full. The account shows Jim Jones, the compassionate healer to be a person of much inward pettiness. Fortson therefore with the ample time at his disposal was not out to slander Jones or to pile offences on his head. He retold a story, which he said Ijames had "shared" with him, and apparently not with Reiterman, a very skilled investigator.

It is the order, reported through Fortson above, given by Jones to a Chris Lewis, known as Teddy Bear, to "bump off" Archie Ijames while the two were on an assignment in the jungle. How can we approach the level of validity of the "unique" report? Teddy Bear was one of those persons in the "doldrums" and rescued by Jones, who put his time at the man's disposal and arranged counselors for him. Teddy Bear had been found not guilty of a murder charge and entered Peoples Temple; Jones had made him, as Fortson would say, a person loving life again. This was compassionate and expert investment by Jones in the human personality, but it was not made without expectations of a return.

Fortson had observed that such people once out of the doldrums felt very grateful to Jones and would do what he asked them to do. It is in this context that Jones required Teddy Bear to "bump off" his elder. Jones had made the assumption that a younger African American of Teddy Bear's challenged background would not have any kind of picture of the highly skilled and disciplined Ijames except as an object Jones wanted removed.

There were other emotions and considerations in Lewis' mind other than gratitude for what Jones had done to rescue him. He did not obey Jones, and, according to Fortson, asked permission to leave to go to the USA to fix up some things and return to stay there forever. Fortson was not clear on the lapse of time between Teddy Bear's departure and the time of his brutal murder on the streets.

Still it was in December, 1977, that the news of his murder was published. Fortson remarked that Jones made a Father Divine-like use of Teddy Bear's death. When a judge who had sentenced Father Divine died suddenly, the messiah had remarked, "I didn't want to do it." This helped to establish his (Jones's) reputation as one not to be trifled with.

Reiterman either does not accept that recollection of Fortson's or does not know of it. Reiterman rather stresses that Jones pounced on Teddy Bear's murderers as enemies of the Temple on the rampage. Both versions may be true as Jones had, according to Fortson, said publicly to Lewis, "I don't want you to go, but if you go something may happen."

Laura Johnston Kohl's Story
Laura Johnston Kohl was in Guyana but not in Jonestown on November 18. Fortson had been sent back to California

from Jonestown to do some important procuring of productive goods.

Ms. Kohl had appeared in the panel at the showing of the film on Jonestown under the auspices of the Jonestown Institute at San Diego State University in July, 2006. She was a ready witness. My wife and I went to her home in Escondido to interview her. She was most forthcoming. We also met her new family: a husband, who is a New Yorker of Puerto Rican descent, and an adopted son, Raul. Raul is of Sikh descent, but was born in the U.S. and was a student at the time of the interview.

She has since written a book of her own (Kohl, 2010) following years of writing on Jonestown and its place in her life and her place in it. She does not moan about the deformations. She is not a weeper. Her book gives glimpses of what white youth are often taught about race. It is worth reading to learn more about the types of people who moved into Peoples Temple. She had been keen on helping friends from Guyana, if she could find them, to migrate to the USA.

Like many others in the Temple, both black and white, Laura Kohl found a sense of release from being able to escape from the racial prison of white or black existence in the USA, only to unknowingly enter into the Guyanese counterpart of African and Indian.

Ms. Kohl had clearly fallen in love with Guyana and may not have left or left so early if November 18 had not happened. Her work there was that of procurer of supplies for Jonestown. She was based in Georgetown. She took orders from Jonestown and found goods in the city and in the countryside needed at the settlement. She clearly enjoyed her work. It took her driving into the East Coast and as far as Berbice, according to her recollection. She readily admitted that Jonestown was never self-sufficient, a fact also confirmed by others.

Rather than ask questions, why don't you tell us your story, just the way you were informally telling me before now.

I first went to Georgetown, Guyana in December, 1974, with a group of about 100 members of the Peoples Temple Planning Commission. We were a group of "worker bees" in the Temple who met with Jim Jones each week to help with the organization as the Temple grew. We stayed in Guyana, including up near the new "Jonestown" community. From the moment I got there, I was in love with the country, the people, and the richness of everything. A simple example: I just loved to see the schoolgirls in their uniforms going to and from school. In the United States, we were an anomaly—we were diverse in racial and economic terms. When we all got to Guyana, we gave a sigh of relief because we were home.

I moved to Guyana permanently in March 1977 as a "procurer." That was my title because I did everything, and in my spare time, solicited donations of anything that could be used in building Jonestown. I purchased sides of beef and pork from the Abattoir, produce from the open markets, shoes from Bata Shoes, machine parts, and drove like a mad woman all around Georgetown. I filled our boat, the Cudjoe, every week with supplies that I bought in Georgetown. I also made many wonderful friends—friends who would invite me to sit down for tea with milk, or delicious curry, or green coconut jelly, or fresh bread. I was delighted each day with my life.

One of my other jobs was to pick up people at the Georgetown airport, and take them through Immigration, and get them to the boat or the airport to get up to Jonestown — 24 hours by boat from Georgetown. I also met people coming in from the Northwest District and took them to doctors, and other appointments. And I cleaned fish to send in to Jonestown, and collected donations of metal scraps and everything I could. One particular friend was the owner of Gooding & Sons, George Gooding. He stayed a wonderful friend to many of us in the Temple until those of us who survived came back to the U.S. He continued to be in touch afterwards, until he died.

After about a year, I was sent into Jonestown. I loved it there as well. Each day, or week, I could see the community flourishing with our hard work. Jim was not around as much as before and we really moved from our allegiance to him, to our love of the community. The children were precious and bright. The rest of us were cared for by our health office, and we were becoming the community of our dreams. Unfortunately, since Jim was not as obvious a part of our lives, we missed the important clues that those close to him watched grow. He was becoming more and more paranoid, crazed, and mentally and physically ill. We had stopped watching him; we were watching the community. His insanity was well-hidden almost all of the time.

I moved into Jonestown after about ten months, from about February of 1978 until the end of October, 1978. Then, Jim asked me to go back into Georgetown to work there. I loved them both and gladly went back into Georgetown. He never called me back in to Jonestown, which is how I survived. When those of us living in the Lamaha Gardens house and the visiting basketball team heard about the deaths in Jonestown, we were as traumatized as the rest of the world. It was a fluke that any of us survived. In Georgetown, one of Jim's closest secretaries took her life and the lives of her three children. The rest of us somehow survived the overwhelming tragedy by putting one foot in front of the other and kept going.

Where were you when the Lamaha Gardens tragedy took place on November 18?

Most of us from the Lamaha Gardens house in Georgetown were at a PNC talent show up the street the evening of November 18. I lived at the headquarters in the city. From there I went into the market to shops and farms, procured fresh goods like fruits, coconuts, vegetables and meats and shipped them to Port Kaituma by the Jonestown vessel.

Any local political activity?

We did participate in a parade in Georgetown, which may have been to support the PNC, but I'm not sure. Tim Carter was in it and may remember. Did you ask Tim or Jordan about PNC activities? They might know more about that aspect. If you want me to, I can ask them to think about it and respond to you directly.

Any dealings with politicians or government officials?

I was not the link between the commune and the government. I dealt directly with Jonestown and with farmers and business places and producers that were suppliers. I did not know any of the political people, but liked the Guyanese and got on very well with them.

Tell me about the self-sufficiency of the settlement.
Up to the time of its destruction it had been dependent on California for manufactured goods including food items and equipment, and on the Georgetown procurement center for Guyanese-produced food supplies.

Any unusual activity at the Lamaha Gardens site?
I had noted the visits to the headquarters of a number of officials. There was one I did not trust. He had a relationship with one of the women of Peoples Temple. Beyond that, it was business as usual.

Why is it that so many forward-looking and highly-motivated people tolerated Jim Jones and all his manipulation?
You see, Jim was saying all the right things. It was only one more case of the use or abuse or rhetoric in political and other endeavors. For me, I was not a gullible person, beyond the fact of believing in Jim Jones as a revolutionary. I had spotted some of his weaknesses but did not feel threatened.

Neva Sly Hargrave's Story

Neva Sly Hargrave had left the Temple around 1974 but like most others not its dreams and its practice of service. Her son (Mark Sly) and ex-husband did die in Jonestown. I did not do a normal one-on-one interview with her, so I am relating and putting together the essential things she told me.

Neva Sly Hargrave spent eight and a half years in Redwood Valley. What attracted her was Jim's compassion, his ability to get people off drugs and his care for children. There was an absence of insecurity, and they all helped one another. It was a spirit of friendship and mutual help. She moved in three months after joining. She became totally involved, organizing games and doing fundraising and participating in healing services.

She had charge of nineteen boys who were African Americans. They took good care of one another. They did not let her go out alone. They would warn off suspects with, "she is family," she said. "I love black people. If they sense prejudice, they say it," she told me.

Ms. Hargrave testified that she was spanked at Peoples Temple for smoking. She also worked in the publications department, working eight hours and sleeping eight hours. Often she slept on a mattress in the luggage compartment of the bus. She repeated that she was beaten in the church with a rubber hose. She began to spot changes in Jim Jones. He was becoming paranoid. She looked into his eyes and they were like knives. Ms. Hargrave did not go to Guyana or to Jonestown. An early admirer and passionate worker and activist, she became disillusioned and looked back with some amusement on what they had taken for real, that is, Jonestown. She has the rare facility of laughing at her own illusions.

There is some exchange I ought to record as it shows to me the state of communications within the Temple community and perhaps the extent to which integration had or had not taken place in conditions of censorship. One always has to remember that there was a charismatic and paranoid intelligence present that managed everything including impressions and communications, not only among members but also between what he Jones treated like "interest groups," including husband and wife, lover and friend.

Ms. Hargrave thought that Pastor-Prophet Hue Fortson clearly had been a person attracted to the Peoples Temple because he saw its good works as consistent with the social gospel of the Christian literature, if not of the church. He had his own expressed opinion of the elder Pastor Archie Ijames. I asked Laura Johnston Kohl one day what she thought of Archie Ijames. She clearly did not see him in the same light as Fortson did. Yet this was a cleric who had followed Jones from Indiana and had given Jones nothing but good, or at least well-intentioned, advice.

Stephan Jones and Don Beck

I would like to mention the two other persons whose words and deeds reinforce my thinking that the American ideals may have been possible to realize abroad with a brand new beginning.

Stephan Jones—This author met Stephan Jones, Jim Jones's biological son, at an anniversary gathering of survivors and friends held in or near San Diego. I have not tried to interview him although he is one of the most interesting figures. Because of his relationship to Jones as a son and because of all he experienced and his principled stands in relation to his father, it seems to me unfair to wring testimony from him. He has been very free in his conversations with authors. I respect him. His mother must have been a saint, and at the same time a prisoner of her own devotion to his father.

Don Beck—Don Beck was a teacher by profession and became a member of the Temple. He visited Jonestown during vacations from school teaching and saw a lot of the positive side of the movement. In my interview with him he was very forthcoming. He typed out, analyzed, and uploaded the diary kept by Edith Roller. She was believed to be an ex-CIA person, but this was never proved. In any case she was converted to Peoples Temple and kept a careful log of developments. She perished on November 18. Much of Beck's testimony therefore is reported on the "Alternative Considerations of Jonestown and Peoples Temple" website of San Diego State University (Moore, n.d.).

What the examples of individuals like those interviewed from among the survivors reveal without a doubt is this: one of the practical aspects of the Temple's move to Guyana was the actual building of community of white and black citizens of the USA, thus raising a model for solving the problem of race in the United States, but doing so abroad.

Father Divine's Peace Mission

I would like to conclude this chapter by looking briefly at the Peace Mission movement in the USA. This group may also be viewed as attempting to solve the race problem, but this time, at home.

The standard bearer of an egalitarian model was the Peace Mission of Father Divine, which made the same attempt at home. Jim Jones had taken anti-racist position from his youth in his native city. The inspiration he took from the Peace Mission was one of bold and open anti-segregated dwelling and one of scale. The Peace Mission did not teach or indoctrinate against race but proclaimed equality for all, carried out anti-segregation policies in its investments and the peopling of its hotels or *heavens*. It survived the glare of an investigative press which on occasion published adverse testimony challenging the Father's profession of sexual abstinence.

While the Peoples Temple under Jones took some symbolic elements from the Peace Mission, its transfer was far more interventionist. Father Divine stayed above the fray until the moment for the judgment seat arrived. Even the exposures did him little significant harm. He was God and carried himself with a divine air, whereas, in the Temple, adherents were expected to handover their wealth as the early Christian believers did according to the Acts of the Apostles. And many got into management of the organization through officers handpicked by Jones, professing and advocating "apostolic socialism."

In the Peace Mission, adherents with money were encouraged or sweetly directed to make joint investments in hotels which they themselves incorporated and then affiliated with the Peace Mission and turned over to the Mission for regulation and for black and white integrated occupation.

Sara Harris (a former Peace Missioness) has written at firsthand about the class/race structure of the Peace Mission Heavens (Harris and Crittenden, 2011). These were in first class hotels acquired by mainly white investors in companies they registered to be occupied in Peace Mission lines. Apparently the ownership issue never arose or became a point of conflict according to the literature surveyed. However public authorities in New Jersey and elsewhere intervened to discourage interracial amity policies. One judge varied the will of the wealthy Mrs. Lyon, whose bequests showed preference for black churches and individuals. Contrary to all he got his believers to expect, Father Divine died from natural causes in 1965, after three full decades of the mission he founded.

The surviving followers found new inspiring leadership, which developed a "new theology," without God present. When Sara Harris investigated some Heavens in 1970, five years after the passing of the immortal Father Divine, she found it active, living with gender segregation, banqueting and sustaining the remaining population but refusing to expand. Harris found that the main body of white believers was rather well-to-do professionals and business people; whereas, the bulk of the down-and-out or — at least the working class — were African Americans. This might have been a generalization. It is likely the ascent of a black God accepted by all for worship took some of the alienation and indignity away from African descendants and, at the same time, relieved the conscious whites of the oppression of guilt for enslavement, Jim Crow, segregation and discrimination.

Attempting to solve the U.S. race problem abroad in the Jonestown project presented some important departures from the selected model, specifically, planting their model community in a strange land.

In both cases (Peace Mission and Peoples Temple) the population was of two main races, then living a conflicted existence in the USA but not in their organization. From the African-American point of view, white Peoples Temple members did not show anything like the incidence of wealthy individuals as Sara Harris found in the Peace Mission. Those who were not working people were far from wealthy and perhaps were breakaway middle class radicals, with a handful of working professionals and anti-racist individuals. Researchers have claimed that, in the case of Peoples Temple in Jonestown, much of the working capital came from the Social Security benefits of the qualified U.S. citizen members, a large proportion of whom were of African descent. Reiterman estimated that some forty thousand dollars [it is more like $36,000] from the U.S. Social Security Department reached Jonestown residents each month in the form of benefit payouts.

Jonestown, a community of mixed black and white individuals like the Peace Mission *heavens* was however headed by a white U.S. citizen, Mr. Jim Jones. They had originated in a wider society of the USA marked by racial inequality. In an ethnically conflicted atmosphere, it will be idle to ask whether these beneficiaries had any control of their benefits, which were enough to overpay for their food and lodgings in Jonestown. The person of highest and unchallenged authority in the Peace Mission was Father Divine, a black man who chose to disclaim race. His presence at the top at least symbolically resolved much of the ethnic insecurity of the society as a whole, at least within the affairs of the Mission. That being so, the number of whites or blacks who were assigned to important tasks became less important than if the head had been white. There was no credible report of any group of whites organizing to reduce the standing of the black angels or to discredit Divine for policies that were too popular, or too much concerned with hunger and homelessness. Though his personality and manner rested on an assumption of divinity, and though he did not escape occasional allegations of ethical breaches, these did not take root or discredit him. Eventually, scholars and eminent social workers like Dr. John Henrik Clarke and Claude McKay regarded him and the Mission as playing an important social and political role.

In Peoples Temple Jonestown the intelligentsia was white. The conclusion must be drawn that although Jones and the Temple interacted with African Americans holding political office, neither members of the intelligentsia, the political leadership types, nor the ingrained working class types were attracted to long term membership of the Peoples Temple. They did not show up in the leadership.

To its credit a large number came from the ranks of the needy, those tired of segregation, or in economic need, and those with a past of handling by the criminal justice system, of addiction or hopelessness. Unfortunately those African Americans ready to play significant roles were not allowed to do so. Archie Ijames lost faith when he was told almost on hitting the ground at Jonestown as man in charge that he would be replaced. Perhaps this replacement had more to do with the buddy feeling than with race, but it had a race effect. According to Reiterman's *Raven ...,* Ijames expressed dissatisfaction. Moreover, Ijames had not flattered Jones when rebuke was needed and these messiahs are usually jealous gods on their own. Father Divine named himself "Jealous" to proclaim this attribute.

Then there was Rabbi Washington (refer to Section V, Appendix and Miscellany, under "People"), who didn't go to Guyana to solve U.S. race problems abroad. He went there for sanctuary, received it, and was made to pay with his reputation. His activity had nothing to do with the progress of the African-American liberation movement. In this he was almost alone. Other African Americans came to Guyana and settled, carried out valuable work in teaching, some of them as aides to the then-Prime Minister Mr. Burnham. Some came from the East Uhuru School of New York to practice nation building and were wholly inoffensive. Zolili and Mamadou as well as Shango and others like L. Massimini from South Africa took part in the Pan African Secretariat's mobilization of the region. Some are mentioned in articles and interviews.

Yet, the collapse of Jonestown was not due to its complacency on the race question, but, if to any one cause, the morbid attachment of the messiah or maximum leader's monopoly of policy and his identifying his own personal issues with those of the commune. He saw a child custody case involving him as a defeat of Jonestown's and the Temple's cause. Instead of deciding on a line of response to that private matter, he ordered revolutionary group suicide.

Chapter 2

Out of the Depths, a Dignity Movement

Interview with Lela Howard

Eusi Kwayana

In this report, Lela Howard tells the story of her aunt Mary Pearl Willis, who perished in the November 18, 1978, tragedy. Lela was just 7 years old when the tragedy occurred. Parts of the story Ms. Howard related to me were in writing and other parts were given over the phone. I have tried to stay as close as possible to her own words in this retelling by me.

Lela Howard has never forgotten her aunt nor her childhood memories. Now a wife and mother, she is able to more fully interpret those early experiences as a child. She has set up a website in her aunt's honor and plans to do good works in her name.

The aunt was Mary Pearl Willis of Louisiana. Young Lela Howard had seen the Rev. Jim Jones when she accompanied her aunt on visits to his church in Los Angeles. She said, "It is hard to call it a church." Her young mind was silently revolted at the open man-worship she thought she saw and heard.

"I still remember him sitting on a chair and everyone was

singing praise and worship songs like 'I love Jim'," said Lela. "My mother who had also accompanied my aunt, on seeing what was going on, said, 'What! My sister, I am leaving right now'."

Lela relates that as she and her mother were trying to leave, people were trying to prevent them from leaving. These people were eyeing Jim Jones, who waved his hand indicating that they could leave. Guards, 20- to 30-year-old, and perhaps even as young as 18 or 19, blocked the exits. These were all black men.

Lela's cousin also attended Peoples Temple but was uncomfortable. Peoples Temple workers took down her aunt's daughter's driver license number. Clearly they were an organized group. They tried to isolate members from their families. She experienced this. Another aunt was also a member for a time, but she left. After that intimidation followed. They used all sorts of tactics to force people to remain members.

Lela felt cheated by her aunt's passing. "I feel cheated that she is not here. She has never seen my son. I try to relay her spirit to him."

When they first moved to Los Angeles, Lela lived with her aunt Mary. They moved into a Peoples Temple apartment building. Lela recalls, "It was a creepy, uneasy feeling. I sure have that sixth sense. I always felt uneasy."

She says that her aunt was only thirty-seven. Imagine that! She was there only three months, going there in August, 1978.

The congregation in Los Angeles was mostly black. It reminded her of a southwestern Baptist church singing Pentecostal, joyful music.

In the late sixties many blacks were trying to be treated equal. They wanted to flee injustice and find respect. Little did they suspect that he, Jim Jones, also wanted to control them and their lives. They turned over everything to Peoples Temple. Why? The way they were persuaded was "I do this for you, you do this for me."

There were not many whites in that congregation that I saw at Los Angeles, said Lela. Most members were from the South and grew up in a segregated environment. They were in search of equality. Yes, the Temple had intimidators. They truly existed. When she first left Louisiana her aunt Mary Pearl Willis was about twenty-five or twenty-six. In fact, at that time the state was segregated in all but name, though not in law.

Lela was soon to learn that this was not a mere historical note, as will become clear below. Ms. Lela Howard, niece of the late Ms. Mary Pearl Willis, still reeling from the tragedy, was troubled and restless and came to a point when she felt called upon to do something in honor of her aunt's memory.

As the reality and largeness of the Jonestown crime and her own under-served loss grew on her, she felt the need to act. She started calling the authorities in the city of Monroe (state of Louisiana) by phone, as she promised herself to mark her aunt's resting place.

She wrote: "Alarm seized hold of me, alarm and disbelief when the authorities told me that the grave was not only unmarked, as I had known, but, as I could not imagine, that the relevant authorities had no plan or map of the cemetery on which the grave had been plotted. After several calls from me and many evasive answers from the city officers, I filed a complaint with the Governor Kathleen Blanco because the city failed to document the grave of a human being. This abuse of authority jolted my sensitivities as a Christian humanist. The elected official Kathleen Blanco soon assigned an officer to directly pursue the search complaint and the required search."

At this point there is other than a private recollection; there is the local press. A reporter at *NewsStar.com* began reporting on the saga. It lasted from March 28, 2007, tracing these experiences from cold denial to refreshing rediscovery. It reports on March 28, 2007, as follows:

> Early today Mary Pearl Willis' niece, Lela Howard, of Culver City, Calif., met with representatives of the city of Monroe and the Louisiana Cemetery Board at Monroe City Cemetery to look for the grave. Following a two-hour search that included discussion with relatives and eyewitnesses, Howard believes her search is over.

According to *NewsStar.com*, Howard's search had begun in October, 2006, when she inquired from Monroe's Public Works Department whether there were any restrictions on placing a headstone on her aunt's grave. She was told that the grave could not be found and nothing could be done about it. It was the elected governor's response to Howard's complaint that got things rolling.

The ensuing search attracted key helpers. The *NewsStar.com* report of March 28, 2007, continues:

> Howard was able to narrow the search area with the help of her cousin Isiah Woods of Monroe. Woods had attended the funeral in January, 1979, and was able to identify the site by the existence of two trees and a concrete border several feet from the burial site.

Herbert Harris, a resident of Monroe, had knowledge of which parts of the cemetery were used in the late seventies. After talking with a woman in Atlanta who had attended the Willis funeral, he was certain of the vicinity. Lela had early decided to press for excavation of a likely area. On March 30, 2007, the *NewsStar.com* reported:

> After a six month search to find the grave of Mary Pearl Willis, it took less than half an hour to excavate a site believed by city officials and Howard to be Willis' final resting place .... "It's done," said an emotional Howard, pointing to her aunt's grave. "She's there and she will be recognized from now on."

The final verification rested on the testimony of Howard, who had told the officials her recollection of the color of the casket she had seen housing her aunt's body. She had told the officials that the casket was of a blue type color with a steel strip on the side.

An official was overseeing the excavation. As workers shoveled the last few inches of dirt from a portion of the grave, Howard broke down in tears. MacFarland, a government official who oversaw the excavation, looked at the color of the casket. "This is the one you described," he said.

There is another side of this episode making it more remarkable. When Ms. Howard first began to visit the Monroe cemetery, she soon discovered that there were in fact two of them, one well cared for and the other allowed to grow to bush and neglect. Early in her search she discovered that she was presuming her deceased aunt to be a trespasser. Her aunt's proper cemetery was the one for blacks, unequal and separate even in death. Here there were no plot maps until the 1980s; hence, the difficulty of locating the Jonestown victim, Mary Pearl Willis, whose name had gone around the world.

She had left Louisiana to escape segregation, found respite as she thought in the Peoples Temple and Jonestown, and after the death she might not have consented to, was returned to a segregated resting place, unmarked and unrecognized, thanks again to the leader of the Peoples Temple.

Her niece Lela Howard, a mother, could not let the experience lapse into sluggish forgetfulness. It sparked her to found a dignity movement: *The Mary Pearl Willis Foundation*. Its inspiration was Howard's simple, powerful resolution. "No matter how it ended," the niece said, "every life matters and should be recognized."

Speaking from its own website, the Foundation works to bring respect and recognition to victims of violence. Mainly it seeks to mobilize comfort and recognition for those who might suffer the fate that threatened her dear aunt and her precious memory. Jim Jones's slogan and appeal on the last night, "Die with dignity," had achieved the opposite. That opposite had to be undone.

Footnote: The website and foundation appear to no longer exist.

I   Members & Survivors

II   Residents & Visitors   ✓

III   Analysts & Critics

IV   Editor & Compiler

V   Appendix & Miscellany

Chapter 3

As Seen by Bystanders

Desmond Andrews, Ayinde, Keith Scott, Suzanne Shukuru
Copeland Sanders, and Kenneth Jones

Eusi Kwayana

Below I list comments from interviews and recollections from individuals who had no stake in the tragedy at Jonestown, but who in the course of their work and their lives stumbled on things still in their memories. It is a bit like going back to the scene of a street accident to see whether tire marks or other evidence have endured. These persons felt no need to hide their identities. The words are their own, in some cases verbatim, and in other cases I am reporting them as told to me.

Desmond Andrews
Medical Auxiliary (as told to Eusi Kwayana)
Mr. Desmond Andrews, a former Guyanese public servant, provided in 2008 a fitting prologue, not the official one, for the entry of Jonestown into the Guyana story. This is one of the interviews which appear in this work. These interviews might not be earth-shaking, but they allow the average Guyanese to witness the making of our history.

As a medic he was doing his health monitoring and surveys related to disease control in the Northwest District (NWD) of Guyana some time in 1973, a year he easily recalls.

One morning, he came upon six visitors at the house of the District Commissioner[1] at Mabaruma on the river. Perhaps they came upon him. They were an unusual group of foreigners, three whites and three blacks. He does not claim that any of them was Jim Jones. One spoke for the group.

"We want to find a place to build a commune here, one that will have no walls, no barbed wire and exclude no one," the spokesperson said. "It will be wholly natural."

The men had a map with them. They left Mabaruma soon after by speedboat for Yarakita. When they returned to Mabaruma around 6:30 p.m., Mr. Andrews was still there in the neighborhood.

The encounter had taken place at the house of the District Commissioner. This type of house is very well known in Guyana's outposts and used to be all painted in a uniform color, the typical government colors. The outpost houses were well protected with mesh at the doors and windows to control mosquitoes.

From what Mr. Andrews found out, the visiting party had come from Georgetown and was staying somewhere in Light Street. City acquaintances had heard that these men had gone to the Northwest and had gone to Kaituma. In case any reader wonders how one man could pick up all this information, let it

---

[1] *District Commissioner: A government official in charge of an administrative district in Guyana.*

be said that strangers, even Guyanese strangers in the Northwest or any interior area, which is reached only by river or air, are news. In those days, the presence of white men [in the NWD] would be bigger news still. And the news becomes the talk of the place. People compare notes, analyze the motives of the visitors and yet are generally friendly towards them.

Before that encounter, Andrews says a satellite had appeared over Moruca one night. It was spotted at Mabaruma, the small market town and administrative center, between 8:45 p.m. and 9:00 p.m. People saw it traveled at full speed, and then stopped, and then sped off again. Very much later it emerged that Jim Jones had radio communication with the USA and was in touch with his headquarters in San Francisco.

Mr. Andrews also said what was previously said by Mr. de Caires, a native NWD resident: that Jonestown people, after the settlement had been established, were often in the Kumaka market selling goods they had brought in from the USA, including radios, tapes and clothing.

The relations between the later Jonestown vendors and the people were friendly. There was one incident reported. A woman vendor from Jonestown made an offer to buy an indigenous child from her mother, and the mother was not amused.

Guyana abounds in dreamers. It will be unfair to omit this part of Mr. Andrews' testimony. This retired public servant told me that he had a premonition about Jonestown, without knowing what it meant. Just two weeks before November 18, 1978, he had a strange dream. He was still working in the Northwest District when he had disturbing dreams. In them he saw a large number of people. He said they were behaving normally. Then suddenly they disappeared and numerous graves appeared in the same location.

It happened that the prime minister of Guyana was then visiting the Northwest and was with a government official. The dreamer told them of his dream. Two weeks later, the news of Jonestown broke.

Mr. Andrews believes that he inherited this dreamer's gift from his grandmother.

Ayinde
Communications Specialist

The Diploma of Public Communication certification at the University of Guyana (UG) required that students attend a practical session in broadcasting at Radio Demerara (RD), the broadcasting studio located in Georgetown, every Saturday morning for a stipulated length of time. Each session started at 10: 00 a.m. and was conducted by Rafiq Khan, General Manager at RD and Lecturer at UG.

About the same time every Saturday, RD would broadcast live a talent show, the name of which I do not remember. On one occasion a band from the Peoples Temple performed.

Uncharacteristically, Mr. Khan allowed us to listen in on the rehearsal. I remember that there were young people, mostly whites but with significant numbers of blacks, maybe in their twenties in that band. The band sounded better than any of the local bands at the time. This, on reflection, suggests that the band either had more sophisticated instruments or had more time to practice or both. During the conversation in my University of Guyana class, it was revealed that the members were located somewhere in Sophia, and that they also played a lot of basketball. At the time Guyanese were not into basketball, so I assumed that they played among themselves. I never heard of the band playing anywhere else. It is possible that it played for official government functions and that is a possible area of research. I never heard of this band afterwards, but we country boys never knew the happenings in Georgetown.

Some years after the incident of November 18, 1978, I spoke with Neville Annibourne, a classmate in the program and a journalist with the Ministry of Information. Annibourne, representing the government ministry, had accompanied the U.S. delegation to the interior. He stated quite clearly that he was certain that the gunmen from the Temple had no intention of injuring any Guyanese on the trip. Their efforts were concentrated on the foreign delegation, especially the congressman. He said that they, the Guyanese, were in plain sight and could easily have been killed. This is at the airstrip after U.S. Congressman Leo Ryan had spoken to residents at the camp and some had indicated their desire to leave. We never discussed in detail the facts as he saw them that day. He seemed unwilling to do so.

A certain group of the local security forces was on the Temple's grounds shortly after the incident. They left with a lot of U.S. currency. That was the first time I saw so much Yankee dollars and realized the power of "In God we Trust."

Keith Scott
Political and cultural activist
My subjective view of the name Jonestown is that it compromises the sovereignty of Guyana. There never was a Jonestown; the proper and legal name is Port Kaituma. I know this will be

A New Look at JONESTOWN

difficult to get across to the world but at some time Guyanese will have to deal with this fact.

I first heard of Jim Jones in the press when the church in Main Street advertised that he was going to hold a service there, followed by some miracle curing at the service. This was followed by disclaimers from the Catholic Church. As an atheist I had no interest in the activity except that I felt it was just another fad. I forgot the name Jim Jones after that for a long time.

One day my mother said she was going to Jonestown and asked if I wanted to go. Jonestown was located in the Northwest area of Guyana, and I wanted to visit the area to see Matthews Ridge and the townships in that part of Guyana. I agreed to go.

I noticed she had to clear my name with Sharon Amos, who was the public relations lady for Jonestown and worked out of their office in Georgetown. My mother seemed quite familiar with Sharon Amos. Later we drove to Ogle, where I met the others who would be making the trip. There was my mother, and also Dr. Leslie Mootoo, Dr. Balwant Singh (the younger Balwant Singh), Laurence Van Sertima, and two or three others whose names I don't recall at this time. Sharon Amos accompanied us as well. The pilot was my Charlotte and King Street Office landlord and friend, Rohan Sharma, who crashed and died in his plane (in 2010, I think). At the time he was flying for the army.

We arrived at Port Kaituma and a flatbed vehicle transported us to Jonestown. On the way Sharon stood up and began a long speech about the great good things the Peoples Temple was doing for the members and the community and their wonderful socialist experiment. Well, I quickly got fed up and I told her what she was talking was not socialism but Christian communism as found in the New Testament. She was surprised and blurted out how did I come to be on this trip. She however quickly regained herself and we arrived without incident.

It was a gated community and those in the village proper had been alerted as to our arrival. Breaking through the foliage I saw a large clearing with a large cage with a monkey. I think it was the mascot of the village.

Jones's wife and other officials welcomed us. There was a look of all smiles and joy on the faces of all the people we saw. The place was very clean, the pathway well defined, and the buildings all clearly de-marked. There was a mix of old, young and the small. There was no feeling of tension.

While we were being taken around I marveled and remarked to Van Sertima how our group was separated and broken into two and I could not see the others. We could have asked any question of any one; naturally, only perfunctory questions were asked. We saw people working, teaching and occupied in other ways. Then we entered a hall and were fed. Later our hosts took us to our quarters.

Van Sertima and I were impressed with the people and the layout of the place. My mother, however, said to me: "Keith, have you not noticed that everybody is smiling? This is not normal. Something is just not right." She told me I must learn to look deeper into situations. Well, at that time I didn't have a clue about a thing. I just saw a group of happy people who stressed that they did not want to return to the USA.

My mother told me that Jim Jones was unwell and we couldn't see him. His wife Marceline — I think that was her name — checked with us often. I was with Van Sertima and Balwant most of the time during our stay and we were comfortable. The thing about his wife was her eyes. They were searching and she somehow struck me as a tormented person. This is not an after the event observation about her. I just quietly felt that way about her on that visit.

We met Larry Schacht, a Temple doctor. We were told he had performed an operation with a U.S. link up. The drugstore [pharmacy] was well stocked. I saw underground storage of preserved food, etc. I formed the impression that all the leaders were white people but I did not voice my observation to anyone.

I did not see Sharon Amos again, but I heard an endless profusion of praise for Jones at every turn. This was not strange as this is what I expected from these modern churches. The leaders and people were all friendly and each of us was given gifts. I was given peas, and a rag which I still have today.

Van Sertima, Balwant Singh, and I met in a room alone with Larry, Jones's wife, and maybe one or two others. The topic of discussion was poison and snakes. Van Sertima exhibited the snakes he had walked with. (He is Guyanese and was famous as a snake charmer.) Mrs. Jones asked him a lot of questions, as did Larry also. To me it was just another talk. That night they kept a dance for us as we were leaving the next day. We all danced but I would say Balwant had a ball.

The next day on take off the plane hit something and could not fly. Rohan quickly shut down the engines and we had to return to Jonestown. This is the same Rohan who crashed a few years later. On our return the reception was just as good as when we first got there.

A day or two later a second plane came for Balwant, Laurence and me, who had remained behind as another plane had taken the others but could not carry us. The pilot was Chan-a-Sue and on the plane were Sharon Amos's two children, a girl and a boy. They were clever and kept us busy with their school knowledge. They and the people I met were all full of life. I had met Jones's [adopted] son, a black youth and he told me of his team's basketball skills and also that they could take care of themselves. I never give it a second thought. I did ask him whether they had guns. He said yes, but again I felt it was no big thing in the jungle. The only guns I saw were my 38, Laurence's 357, and Rohan's army issue.

A few days or weeks later my mother awakened me at about midnight and told me that at Jonestown right then they were all dying by suicide after killing a congressman. Leo Ryan was in the papers as going to investigate Jones. I was following that. Then I later heard that Sharon and those two nice children had died. There was a young lady, black, married to a white member. She seemed to have been a senior member. She was friendly to us. I saw her in at Rex's[2] office shortly after the events. I engaged her in talk. I asked her if those people I saw could have killed themselves and she said yes. I also asked her if she was there if she would have done the same and she said yes.

---

2   *Rex McKay, a prominent attorney in Georgetown, Guyana.*

Well brothers, this is as comprehensive as I can recall and it is the first time I have written anything on those events. I hope it will be helpful.

Suzanne Shukuru Copeland Sanders
U.S. Citizen working as a Nurse / Midwife in Guyana

For about three and a half years from (Jan 1977 to Jun 1980) I lived in Guyana, South America, where I underwent training to become a midwife and then practiced afterwards as a midwife at Public Hospital Georgetown (PHG). I happened to be there when the tragedy of Jonestown occurred.

I remember being at work at Lady Thompson Ward at the Public Hospital Georgetown (PHG) on the Sunday morning of November 19, 1978, when I received a phone call from a friend, another expatriate from Brooklyn living in Georgetown, who had just heard a news report on the radio about some people, maybe 4 or 5, who had been killed in the northwest area, something related to Jonestown. Later that day she called again to say that the count had gone up to over 20 and then called again to say that unbelievably now it seemed that over 40 people had died. Of course the count proceeded to increase in the next few days.

Guyana did not have television then; all our news came from either radio reports or from friends who had telephone access to family or friends overseas and were getting more complete news information. There was also a very state-controlled newspaper, very strong on sports and social activities but very party-line regarding politics. A very thin international version of Time and Newsweek were also sometimes available. In any case it was not easy to get any reliable up-to-date news regarding Jonestown.

I didn't know a lot about the Peoples Temple. I knew they were a group from California which had established a settlement up in the northwest area of Guyana along the Venezuelan border. At that time the area was sparsely settled and it was very much in the Guyana government's interest to have people up there so it could secure its borders. The government made settling up there very affordable, something like fifty cents per acre. It offered leases for 99 years. This was attractive to some adventuresome individuals or groups seeking to get 'back to the land.'

In fact I was part of a black nationalist organization in Brooklyn, NY, called The East, which sought to put theory into practice and to develop hands-on nation-building skills. This was a natural extension of the East's efforts at institution building. The East had established an independent school called Uhuru Sasa, a food co-operative called Kununuana, a clothing co-operative called Mavazi and several other institutions in addition to its weekly cultural offerings, and political education classes for the community. As an organization we had visited Guyana in 1971 as guests of ASCRIA (the African Society for Cultural Relations with Independent Africa). A few years later we took advantage of the government's attractive invitation to come and settle the land in the Northwest. We established a farm there, near a place called Mabaruma, growing peanuts and selling them back down in Georgetown. It was very convenient for the folks up there that I had a place where they could stay in the city, and it was welcome company for me when they came into town to sell their crops. I only got up there to visit Mabaruma once in all the time I was in Guyana.

Although Jonestown was up in the northwest, the Peoples Temple also maintained a residence in Georgetown. Soon after I arrived in early 1977, I remember that they had an open-house and a friend and I attended. I had the sense that since they were newcomers in a new country they were trying to reach out and be friendly and tell people about Jonestown. I think they showed slides and had a question and answer period. I remember that they had a glossy brochure describing the amenities of Jonestown; a kind of utopian society built and maintained by hard-working folks who provided for elders who could have their blood pressure checked daily and for youths by having a nurturing day care system. The brochure showed photos of a state-of-the-art "theater" meaning an operating room. As a nurse I was impressed in that this group seemed to have facilities that surpassed what we had at the public hospital.

There were perhaps four or five people from our group who stayed up in the northwest, (or 'the bush' as anywhere in the hinterland was called) at any one time. Some stayed for a few years and some for a few months. There was no overland way to get to the northwest. The only way, other than a small prop plane which was very expensive, was the regular boat which left once a week or sometimes every two weeks out of Georgetown and followed the coast westerly up to Port Kaituma.

Often the East brothers (occasionally sisters) traveling to and from the northwest would inevitably be on the boat with members of the Peoples Temple who were traveling up to Jonestown. Since they were also from the States, they would often engage in friendly conversation. The whole trip took about 24 hours. Later I heard that the Peoples Temple got their own boat that was faster than the Guyana boat and that it went directly to the States and back and was allowed to enter and exit without going through Guyana customs.

At some point, maybe towards the end of '77 or the beginning of '78 I remember folks discussing how there seemed to be a very different attitude among the Peoples Temple people. They no longer were outgoing or friendly; they actually withdrew from conversations with outsiders and they no longer invited people to their Georgetown residence. They were sometimes described as paranoid, suspicious or subdued. I believe this coincided with the time when Jim Jones himself started spending more time at Jonestown.

By November, 1978, it was not unusual to hear of vague rumors associated with Jonestown especially regarding [alleged] payoffs to the government to bypass government regulations. Still, the horror of what was to become evident is virtually unmatched in human history. I believe we do not yet know the full story of what really happened there.

A few days after the massacre various government officials and some Guyana Defence Force (GDF) soldiers went up there. A good friend of mine came to visit me after he returned from there and described horrific sights and smells that made him nauseous. He said that in one storeroom near the operating room/clinic he saw boxes and boxes of drugs. He was not familiar with the names but remembered that one was spelled t-h-o-r-a-z-i-n-e. Thorazine is an anti-psychotic drug.

A week or so after Nov. 18, we received some patients at the hospital who had been flown down from the northwest. They had jumped off the runway when the shooting began and hid in the side brush for days, scared to come out even when they saw people because they were not sure who they were. Their wounds had become very infected, and I remember picking out maggots with tweezers. I recall that they stayed for a few days and then were flown back to the States.

In the days following the killings I heard talk about the 'basketball team' that unlike the residents of Jonestown seemed to have the ability to come and go. As I said, I do not know exactly what happened at Jonestown but I firmly believe that we do not yet know the true story. It is very convenient to lay all this at the feet of a so-called madman, but many questions remain unanswered.

It is ironic that I now live in the Bay Area, the home of the Peoples Temple at the time it went to Guyana. I regularly pass the cemetery in Oakland where so many of the believers, overwhelmingly black, had lived. May they truly rest in peace and may the truth of Jonestown someday come to light.

Kenneth Jones
Resident in Jonestown area (as told to David Hinds)
In reply to the first question that according to Dr. Ptolemy Reid in the National Assembly about 14 Amerindian children had perished in the disaster, the informant said deliberately that according to "our information there were about six." The informant had been a businessman in that part of the interior for some years, had been there before the Jonestown settlement and was there after it collapsed. He had credible knowledge of the Kaituma Basin and the whole environment and had no reason one way or the other to spin tales.

"I think the parents had asked them to adopt the children. There were no other Guyanese there," Kenneth Jones said with some confidence.

[He was evidently explaining how the six Amerindian children that perished in the tragedy happened to be in the Temple. There were actually eight native-born Guyanese children who died in Jonestown. About half of that number was adopted or in the process of being adopted. —E.K.]

According to this resident of the Northwest region where Jonestown was located, the community outside of Jonestown never got word of a series of rehearsals for the White Night, the final outcome, before it happened. He said that they got all of that information only after the event. Asked whether or not the Jonestown residents were armed, he said, "They never publicized that." He had never seen Jonestown people with arms.

He said it was not easy to get in there. Jonestown had to know you. Strangers were stopped about a mile off. Then someone would call the settlement for permission. "They had to know you." Kenneth Jones had heard that Jonestown had a boat which they used to bring goods into the country and the commune without customs procedures, thus in breach of customs. He said that whether or not customs procedures were obeyed he would not know. However, it was a fact that their boat did bring goods into the country and reports said that unloading of the cargoes took place at night.

"Boats will get in there at night and then they would unload the stuff or whatever it was at night."

Hinds next moved into the area of inter–community relations and social psychology. He asked whether there was, and if so, to what extent, any suspicion in the communities about what these people were really up to.

A few people had this suspicion, but for the majority, no. "Man," they would tell one another, "the boys come to do agriculture, and you know that they were foreigners and many people still have this thing about foreigners, especially white people."

What was the kind of response when people learned of the tragedy? "Take where you were, what was the response of people to the tragedy when the news broke? And how did you all learn about it?"

Chapter 4

Report of the Agri-Audit Task Force

Lennox Massay, et al.

A few months after the Jonestown tragedy, a fact finding team was sent to the area to assess conditions and make recommendations for the future. This is the report of its investigation, which gives a good idea of the extent of the operations and the efforts to make use of the land and environs. This report is important in that it is an assessment from a non-Temple source. As stated by Peoples Temple member Laura Kohl elsewhere in this book, Jonestown was not self-sufficient — contrary to the claims of its leaders. The original of this document was signed by each committee member.

General
On March 2, 1979 (Friday), a task force comprising of Dr. P. Munroe, Dr. Bacchus, *Cde.* Gibbs, *Cde.* Collins, Capt. Lennox Massay, and Major Henry visited Jonestown in the Northwest District.

The purpose of their visit was to examine the Jonestown complex with the aim of answering the following questions:

1. What were the factors that aided Jones and his followers in their developmental works?

2. Whether or not locals can control the settlement and take advantage of the techniques and technology employed by the foreigners?

3. If the settlement should be continued, what practices might be used for its successful operation?

Possibilities
The party was divided into groups with each group having specific responsibilities. Dr. Munroe and Capt. Massay were tasked with the responsibility of looking into the agricultural aspects of things. This included both crops and livestock.

Constraints
The party reached Jonestown late because of inclement weather conditions and as such had approximately three hours to complete the task. There were much to look at in Jonestown and to make a detailed analysis and assessment of the whole situation would entail spending at least about two or three days.

Location and topography
The farm is situated about six miles west of the Kaituma air strip with a *fair weather road* connecting them.

The area consists of undulating lands with increasing altitude as one travels away from Kaituma. As such, drainage is not a problem.

Vegetation
The area consists of heavy rain forests with canopy in excess of one hundred and fifty feet from ground level. The undergrowth is intermixed and made up mainly of vines and wild bananas.

Soil
The soil is a reddish-brown and sandy clay, the crests of most hills having more sand than clay. When saturated, it is extremely sticky and when dry it becomes very hard. These conditions make it, therefore, very difficult to cultivate in extremes of weather, i.e., in wet weather it's difficult to prepare and in extreme dry weather it is likewise. These types of soil very often need a heavy dosage of limestone and this is particularly so in the Northwest District. It is, therefore, recommended that a detailed soil survey be done in this area to classify the soils.

This can be divided broadly into two areas of the three-mile roadway which starts from the junction of the Port Kaituma/Arakaka and Matthews Ridge roadway to the area in and around the settlements.

Roadway
This three-mile roadway has been cultivated on both sides. The width of the cultivation on each side is approximately 25 yards. The first mile of this roadway is cultivated with bananas and plantains, which are in urgent need of weeding and transplanting to fill the vacant spots. The second mile is cultivated with bitter cassava, the majority of which are ready for reaping. The third mile-stretch has a portion of citrus inter-cropped with bitter cassava. Another portion has pure citrus. Added to this were sugarcane which were planted on

the lower grounds and some sorrel and pineapple also made up the cultivation of the last mile stretch.

Settlement
The crops grown in and around the settlement were bananas, sweet cassava, pineapples, citrus and other fruit trees which included breadfruit, malacca, bilimbi, carambola and cherries. There was evidence to show that peanuts, stringed beans, sword beans and pigeon peas were extensively grown.

There was also evidence to show that legumes mainly stringed beans and sword beans were used as livestock feed. The sword beans were dried and stored in steel drums with special mechanism for moisture control.

Some amount of green vegetables, namely: okra, cabbage, spinach, etc. were grown; most likely, these were for domestic consumption.

There were also approximately seventy five acres of land cleared, prepared and ready for planting.

Livestock area
This area is situated about one and a half (1½) miles from the settlement along the road to Kaituma. The livestock complex is on an area of approximately seventy five (75) acres with much room for expansion. This complex has its own water pump and electrical generating plant.

The following buildings made up the complex:

1. A large bond used mainly for storing grains, fertilizer and other feed stuffs. These included corn, rice, sword

beans, and molasses. Large quantities of food stuffs, e.g., flour, sugar, lard, etc., were also kept there. Part of this bond was used as a cattle and horse shed. Equipment in and around the bond were a shredder used for chopping sugarcane (presumably for feeding to the animals), a corn sheller, a cassava mill, and a cassava juice extractor.

2. Two large piggery buildings, one unoccupied and the other housing one hundred and thirty three (133) pigs comprising boars, sows, fatteners, and piglets.

3. Four or five large poultry houses which we did not examine because of limited time. We were informed that these pens housed one thousand eight hundred young layers. We were also informed that the floor of these pens were made of foam topped with shell and a mixture of sand.

Cattle and horses

There were twenty five cattle and two horses, which grazed on surrounding semi-improved para grass pastures. These were approximately thirty (30) acres of para grass pastures which needed maintenance.

Pigs

The pig pen walls were constructed mainly of hand bound wood and the floors were of hard wood slabs. Fine shells mixed with sand were used on the floor to absorb the urine and feces. This mixture was removed periodically and utilized as manure.

We were informed that the pigs were fed with corn, molasses, cassava tops, copped sugarcane and legumes, supplemented with commercial pig feed.

Comments
Jim Jones and his followers made extensive and good use of native materials, assistance, and technology in the organic stages of the settlement's development.

The forest was cleared with very little damage done to the top soils, and this is a very important factor in converting a forested area into crop lands.

The crop area is now in urgent need of weeding and other husbandry practices. Yet the healthy growth and condition of the crops that exist suggest that the practices adapted by Jones were suited for successful production.

It must be borne in mind that Jones had at his disposal a large labor force which enhanced his position.

We were in no position to determine the type and quantities of fertilizers used.

Recommendations
We believe that this commune would be developed into a thriving agriculture settlement if the following recommendations are followed:

1. A team of specialists needs to visit the site with the aim of formulating an Agricultural Development Program. This team should comprise the following:

- Soil Chemist
- Crop Agronomist
- Agricultural Engineer
- Plant Pathologist
- Entomologist
- Livestock Officer
- Hydrologist

2. Assuming that the team of specialists visits and formulates a feasible program which, if implemented, a farm manager who is very experienced, knowledgeable, and physically fit should be placed in charge. The degree of success or failure of a farm business depends greatly on the type of management it has. In similar fashion a good manager cannot function properly without the necessary supports such as skilled labor and all the other ingredients that go with farm production.

3. Some amount of work should be done on livestock feeds and feeding in the area, because the problem today with livestock is the expensive cost of feeds. The problem is even greater in this area because of poor transportation facilities. Jones started off in the right direction. He recognized the need for cheap feed supply and thus incorporated local materials in his feed stuff, although the corn he used seemed to be imported from the USA.

4. Guyana has enough local materials which could be utilized to satisfy the carbohydrates requirements. Protein needs could be met by legumes and some amount of animal protein to compile a balanced ration for livestock.

5. Work on feeds and feeding for livestock in this area would not benefit Jonestown alone, but could be useful in other areas of the country especially the interior regions where land is readily available and transportation is a real problem.

We do hope that this report satisfies the requirements of the task force and that it will be of some benefit.

Chapter 5

In the Shadow of the Temple

Interview with Lennox Massay

Eusi Kwayana

Lennox Massay was the Agricultural Officer in the Northwest District during the Jonestown era. Part of his work engaged him in close proximity to the Temple area. He did this interview with me in Atlanta in 2006. Subsequently he went back to live in Guyana but had to return to the U.S. for medical treatment. He died of natural causes in 2011. The notations in brackets [ ] are mine and inserted for clarity.

Could the Guyana Defence Force stop the Jonestown massacre? And if they could, why didn't they?

The Guyana Defence Force (GDF), in theory, had the power to intervene in Jonestown and stop the massacre or part of it, in any case, to reduce the death toll. This is what most people believe. Strangely, the Rev. Jim Jones made use of the existence of the GDF, with which he had a close working relationship, to create the state of mind he needed to convince his flock to accept "revolutionary suicide." Jones had praised the Guyana government for not permitting extradition. On November 18, 1978, however, after gunmen from the Temple had killed Congressman

Ryan when a number of dissidents began to follow the visitor out of the commune, Jones felt that the game was up. He felt or argued that because of that incident the government of Guyana was almost bound to dispatch troops to the area. He meanly suggested to the crowd that the Guyana troops would be coming. "The GDF will be here, I tell you. They'll torture some of our children here. They'll torture our people. They'll torture our seniors." These are some of the things he told them.

Mr. Massay, how long have you been in the area, and what has been your experience working not far from the Jones settlement?

We went to Jonestown on a Friday in March, 1979, and we did a survey of what was there. What I am going to do instead of recording it is to leave with you a copy of our report. [See Chapter 04, Report of the Agri-Audit Task Force.]

I was sent to Kaituma to be in charge of the area and to look after the three cooperatives: Key West, West Bank, and Explorers. They were planting peanuts and other crops. I made sure they were doing a good job and everything was going well [with] the peanuts. You [Eusi Kwayana] helped to purchase the peanuts for Guyana Marketing Corporation. You were there at that time. It was going good. And then they came in a group and said, "Mr. Massay, we have decided that we want to leave this place."

I said, "Why?"

They said, "We miss Georgetown."

I said, "How we have arranged it, every couple weeks you all go to Georgetown." They said no, they have missed Georgetown.

During that time there was a gentleman named Mr. Amsterdam who was in agriculture, and I used to get cattle from another area. He used to send me cattle every couple of weeks. And I used to kill the cattle to help to provide them [the residents] food and so forth. So I told Amsterdam there is some land about two miles in from Kaituma that I could use as a place for rearing cattle. It had good soil and so on and so forth.

And that was the same land that was given over to Jim Jones, not knowing that Jones wanted not to be in Kaituma and exposed to the people there; so he went down to the very back to be by himself, and half way through they had cattle and so on.

When I visited Jonestown, the person whom I knew and spoke with doesn't always look like Jim Jones. Like apparently he has somebody who looks like him. I went there a few times with these different groups and so forth. Yes, I advised from time to time. And when the suicides took place, I forget the colonel's name but the captain was Captain Benn, Leroy Benn. They [the GDF soldiers dispatched from Georgetown and destined for Jonestown] tried to land at Kaituma but it was misty. Then they landed at Matthews Ridge and I had to explain to people why there has to be a Supreme Being on this earth. A fellow named Lambert is in charge of the engine of the train. *[The train runs from Matthews Ridge to Kaituma, a distance of about 32 miles. Jonestown is on the way, about 6 miles before Kaituma, on a side road another one and a half miles down. —E.K.]* The main engine broke down. Then the backup engine broke down. And then the reserve engine wouldn't start. Then they [the GDF soldiers] jumped in a vehicle to go to Arakaka,[close to Jonestown], and the bridge was damaged! They had a flood there. So they had to go back to Matthews Ridge. [Thus, they never got to Jonestown in time.]

Was this a plane carrying people to ... was this a plane carrying a load?
No, the plane that carried the soldiers there to stop the suicides.

They blame the army for arriving late but the army arrived at Matthews Ridge, thirty miles from Kaituma and the three engines broke down. So there was no way for the GDF to get to Kaituma except by covering the thirty-something miles by road.

The weather changed at Kaituma. So they couldn't land at Kaituma. They landed at Matthews Ridge. So they had to walk [to Kaituma]. So they arrived after midnight when the suicide death had taken place. Because, according to the survivors, some of them said that after some people began to drink the mixture and they began to realize that it wasn't a good idea, they were shot and some of them were injected. So it was not only the poison. *[Officially only 2 members died of gunshots, one of whom was Jim Jones. —E.K.]*

Others tried to getaway in the surrounding areas. Even though they had a lot of snakes they were able to get away because the bush was very ... you know. Then they had the decision to take the team to investigate. I went in with the team because I knew the area.

On that trip [there were] a lot of people who did not understand. The settlement had some small huts and in those huts you had six double bunks, that is, twelve beds. And then Jim Jones had in a small cabin a little ladder in which you had three single people above so you had an average of 30 people in these small buildings. You had a few large buildings with perhaps the rich persons who were there but most of the people lived in a cramped environment, 24 to 30 in a small building. There was also — this is not in my report — but I met those people [who] said there was something they put into their drink in the afternoon or at night that sort of controlled their activities. The GOG (Government of Guyana) never investigated that part of it. We were told that they were sort of conditioned and in every single hut there were two loudspeakers. Certain time in the night they were being conditioned by not only liquid but by him coming over at a certain time in the night pushing them to a certain way they must follow exactly what he says and so forth.

He was also doing gold. Even though I was in Kaituma, not being a geologist, I never did check on that aspect. But when I checked the map I realized that the place had a lot of gold.

What evidence was there of that?
They found some pits and the pits were covered up. Even that was not exposed to the Guyana public. I don't know if they found gold or if they were doing some exploration but they did have some pits in which there is evidence that

they were looking for gold and so forth. Even right now people are negative about the area, but Kaituma has a lot of gold. Jonestown was a part of Kaituma. He gave it his name. Arakaka was a gold place where they had a big shot. Kaituma is about 12 to 15 miles from Arakaka.

How long were you there?
I was there when you all came up there [some years earlier]. People at Arakaka made a mistake when they were mining gold. They left, and then came the water! And the water washed away … . The miners made a mistake. When they were mining, gold was there and instead of staying there and mining the gold they went to Matthews Ridge and partied and when they came back the whole place was flooded. A lot of people are afraid to group there, because it is a very dangerous area with water. But you have to have a lot of control of the rivers. I still feel that even now the government should revisit that area and see where they could settle 125 people instead of people just staying in Georgetown.

You never can tell what will happen with the seepage. I was in Guyana in 2004. When I went up to Sophia and I saw the seepage about 40 feet below. I spoke with the Indian man, the people who were doing the development there for the Caribbean Secretariat. I said to myself let me go and tell Robert Corbin [Leader of the Opposition] and Bharrat Jagdeo [President of Guyana] that they are going to have a flood. I left before the flood came, but think I was wrong in not doing it because as a Christian I should have told them that because of the seepage, when the water comes in from the ocean it doesn't [stop].

You mean it runs into a high water table?
You've got it. High water table. So because of a high water table and that is why I have a report at home, which I may have to send for you in which Sir Godfrey Evans had written about the resettlement of Guiana. He said that Makouria was a high ground and you could place the capital there. You could then approach the capital from the West Bank road and from the Parika road. It was a twenty-year plan.

I knew the Evans report. Please continue.
You have to start to move inland in some respect. If you have any friends who want to go into ranching they can use the Berbice River for ranching.

Back to the report on Kaituma, it is very sad that that took place, especially when we wanted to have settlements in these areas and to get people to move away. Hamilton Green [Senior Minister of the Government] was one of the main persons who started those cooperatives at Port Kaituma.

Chapter 6

The Peoples Temple and the Guyana Government

P. D. Sharma

[This article is valuable as it was written by a poet, scholar, and citizen who had observed the coming of the Peoples Temple to Guyana and visited its commune at Jonestown. It was also written within a few weeks of the Jonestown massacre. —E.K.]

How did Jim Jones choose Guyana, a place so remote and so virtually unknown? Instincts confirm a close and definite relationship between the Peoples Temple and the government of Guyana, but material evidence has so far eluded investigations.

On more than one occasion Jim Jones said that he was attracted to Guyana by the government's philosophy of "Feed, House, and Clothe Yourself." The pastor cited biblical passages purporting that the feed-house-and-clothe-yourself business of the Guyana government was what God ordained for man. At the outset, from introducing his movement in that way, he was perceived as a fraud by quite a few people in Guyana.

However, the Guyana government endorsed the Temple as a model cooperative group—just what the Guyanese nation as a whole was aspiring to become. Cooperativism was the chosen philosophy of the government, not capitalism, socialism, communism, or Marxism, which brands already had their trademarked established owners in Guyana.

All of this began five years ago. The house-feed-and-clothe plan was beginning to expire (while still in draft). A new slogan—Produce or Perish—was taking its place. And Jim Jones and his flock are now in the horror pages of history.

Controversial persons coming to Guyana were nothing new. The investment reaped great political dividends in that it contributed to the radicalization of the image of the Guyana prime minister. In 1970 at a Conference of Black Revolutionary Nationalists and Pan-Africanists hosted in Guyana, at which the media was barred, the prime minister promised asylum to African freedom fighters as well as Afro-American freedom fighters. This stance, among others, pretty well established the prime minister of Guyana as a black ally and friend to black revolutionaries worldwide. When no sister Caribbean country would accept Stokeley Carmichael on a speaking tour, Guyana did.

As a result quite a few black Americans came to Guyana, if not to live and work, just to visit and proselytize. Julian Mayfield, former advisor to Ghana's Kwame Nkrumah, was at one time the closest advisor to Guyana's prime minister. Muhammad Ali was on his way, but didn't make it from Trinidad. I was unofficially told that his finding out that the Guyana dollar was worth .50 U.S. cents was one of the reasons for his canceling out of the contract. *[At time of this publication the Guyana dollar is worth 0.0048 U.S. cents. —E.K.]*

A black American group called the Uhuru Sasa was secretly given lands to settle and farm. Unlike the Peoples Temple they had no assets and the Guyana government extended to them enormous material assistance. Local residents in the community told me that Uhuru Sasa members were planting something they never saw before and that they protected it like gold. The thing seemed to take the Guyana soil quite well too. The government was giving all this support in hush-hush fashion and the public was never fully informed about it.

[Uhuru Sasa (Swahili for 'Freedom Now') is a black freedom school in Brooklyn. Its members say they received land at a cheap rental and were not otherwise supported by the government of Guyana. —E.K.]

Perhaps the most well-known black American to have come to Guyana is David Hill, who fled the U.S. while his appeal against conviction for blackmail was being heard. He now goes by the name Rabbi Emanuel Washington and heads the all-black House of Israel group. They see themselves as Black Jews, a designation that engendered both curiosity and bewilderment. The East Indian community sees it as a cult clandestinely supported by the black government to confront members of East Indian descent at the rank level of race. The government claims that under the freedom of religion act the House must be permitted to function. "This is not a Christian country," the prime minister said, "this is a religious country." The same play of words was used in defending *obeah*, a black arts practice the Christian community wanted outlawed. A government statement read, "Obeah will not be legalized, but its practice will no longer be illegal."

[While the term 'obeah' was attached to the practices of some unofficial African religious practitioners, magic itself had no such confines. The Hindu versions of it were called Jaadu or obeah. 20th century history records the cases of Molly Shultz and Lillowattie. The first was a fatality of pseudo Hindi magic and the second of pseudo African magic, both legally classified as obeah. —E.K.]

With black men and black movements there was much the government could gain politically. Not so with the Peoples Temple whose leadership was white and suffered from constant allegations of extortion and corruption. From any angle, given the reputation of the Peoples Temple, close association was bound to be embarrassing for the government.

When Jones first came to Guyana in 1973 he launched his Peoples Temple with great fanfare and heraldry. He kindled the kind of religious fervor the Guyanese people were accustomed to expect from American evangelists. He borrowed the ornate Sacred Heart Cathedral belonging to the Catholic Church and announced his coming in an event that was rehearsed to theatrical precision.

This writer was present at the ceremony and can still remember portions of his sermon. "Have faith. It is faith that will heal you. Faith is everything. You do not have to be educated to have faith; in fact, if you are educated, that can be a hindrance to having faith."

Every major exhortation was laced with a chorus saying, "Amen! Amen!" and some musicians beating Boom! Boom! The M.C. (more like a D.J.) sounded like John the Baptist preparing the way, and Jones was on top all the way. From soul raising pulpit eloquence Jones would come down to the level of the floor with quips like: "I only have one pair of shoes; why should I have more when I only have one pair of feet."

A few "miracles" were performed. Blood-looking stains remained on the white blouse of a woman from whose inside a malignant something was removed. The something looked like fresh chicken liver to me.

All in all, the affair was a performance to be applauded — the con notwithstanding. People were literally leaping on top of each other to touch Jim Jones, who teased them with a dramatic walk down the aisle. I remember an old crippled woman in perspiration and pain being arduously propped up by relatives to get in front while the able-bodied kept pushing forward.

My wife implored me to hurry home and bring her wheel-chaired mother. I caught a student of mine, who was noted for his athletic agility, in a horizontal position literally swimming on the heads of people to get closer. And Jones, exploiting reverse psychology, exhorted them: "Touch me not; it is faith that will heal you. Believe and you will be cured."

The culture of Guyana made a man like Jones and a movement like Peoples Temple especially attractive. People from outside Guyana need to be reminded that Guyana has no television and there is only one main road. Everything happens in person and on the spot. True theater in Guyana consists of political orations and, to a lesser extent, religious sermons. People in attendance at a political or religious rally to be addressed by the leader (usually a messianic one) usually experience and take away something transcendental.

After that controversial inauguration, virtually nothing was heard about the Peoples Temple again. Its relations with the Guyanese people were never too close, nor too distant. The reporter who said that they were neither strangers nor friends to the local population was accurate. Temple members kept to themselves like an outlawed fraternity.

The author took this shot of his investigating team standing outside the benab of the Peoples Temple. L to R: Marcellus Agrippa, Mahendra Dutt, Nedira Sharma, Guyanan Sharma, and Ainsley Noble.

There are instances of Guyanese men trying to date Temple women without success. There seems to have been an artificial bar placed on mingling with the local people. To think that so many people could live in a foreign land without a few instances of romance developing between guest and host is indeed somewhat strange.

Yet the Temple folks at Jonestown objected when I referred to them as Americans. They said they were now Guyanese. The government's political party office in the region had sometimes received "complaints" from Jonestown members that they were not invited to participate in community affairs as much as they would like to, now that they were an integral part of the country.

Other contacts the Guyanese people had with Temple members took place when they sometimes offered their produce for sale at the market square and when they solicited donations from businesses and wealthy individuals. Guyanese knew that these were token acts with ulterior designs. So too were the bits of campaign work they did on behalf of the ruling political party.

The question Guyanese really wanted to know was what precisely was going on in the secluded and sealed off camp that is Jonestown. Only a handful of local people lived in that district which is about 150 miles away from the capital city and connected, for the most part, only by air transportation. To them Jonestown was a strange and disturbing presence in their midst.

At nights gun shots would be heard in a pattern which ruled out hunting or target practice. While the rest of the community slept, small aircrafts would land at the old airstrip and be unloaded and loaded. Jones used two tractors to give illumination and guidance to the pilot. Also, vessels would dock and two tractors would come to transport their cargo.

Dark forebodings came upon the Guyanese around Jonestown as to what really was going on inside the commune. Out of the mystery rumors grew and questions began to be asked. That the district (PNC) party chief could not answer these questions and that he himself was in the dark as everybody else confounded the residents. Doubtlessly he must have asked questions from the central party office in Georgetown and still no answers came.

The alarming nature of this development and its grave implication can only be appreciated with some understanding of the nature of Guyana politics.

The philosophy of the Guyana government is embraced in the phrase, "Paramountcy of the Party." This is a doctrine which stipulates that the party is supreme over the government and the state. A corollary doctrine is that of the Maximum Leader—this holds that the ruler is greater than the flock. On close examination the affinity between the Peoples Temple and the government of Guyana is to be found in the identity of their principles, not in any feed-house-and-clothe-yourself camouflage.

Nowhere in Guyana is the paramountcy of the party principle better entrenched than in the Northwest District region which comprises mainly Port Kaituma, Matthews Ridge and Jonestown. The leader of the East Indian Party whose racial representation accounts for about 50% of the overall population (the ruling black party accounts for about 40%) could not even get a car to drive him around in the area because no one dared to be seen in the company of the enemy, even for legitimate non-political business.

It is no exaggeration to say that in that region the party is higher than the government and the state. And that the

Peoples Temple could operate outside the party meant that it got its carte blanche *directly from above*—an expression used in Guyana to denote the fountain and source of all power, Prime Minister Forbes Burnham.

Here again one must explain what is meant by power in a country like Guyana. The U.S. President, the British Prime Minister, the German Chancellor and the Japanese Emperor combined do not have more power within their respective domestic confines than the power the prime minister of Guyana has in his. In most third-world countries the situation is the same. It is not unusual for a head of a third-world country with as much power within as lack of influence without to muse to himself when thinking of his counterparts in developed world: they can spend more than I but they can't rule more than I.

Besides power, in their insistence on obedience, in the pleasure they derived from ego gratification, in the way they stage-manage appearances, Jim Jones and Forbes Burnham make strange bedfellows. Indeed Jim Jones's reputation for wheeling and dealing is outmatched by that of Burnham's. One is reminded that he [Burnham] is credited with the statement that politics is the science of deals and alliances—a definition worthy of status among the greatest thoughts in political philosophy.

Deals—and particularly political deals—are the highest form of what is referred to as a gentleman's agreement. They defy ocular proof. The very terms of the deal cater for avoiding discovery, revelation and proof. Thus, in investigating the possibilities of a deal, credibility and not proof is what is at issue.

Jones's background is well known and well publicized. It is a history of hypocrisy and deviousness. The man seems to have a talent for getting close to high personages and capitalizing on the contact. That he was capable of being a party to a deal with Burnham is not only possible but well nigh likely. On the Burnham side of the coin we find a career no less immersed in the cloak-and-dagger.

Forbes Burnham is a lawyer by profession, which in itself says something. In Guyana and indeed many other countries the legal profession is not a haven of virtue and righteousness. "Me never had to tek lawyer yet" is a common declaration of Guyanese to profess a life free of strife and acrimony. And to have to hire a lawyer is generally felt to be a more dreadful thing than the crime that required doing so.

That the CIA helped Burnham get into power, replacing the Marxist premier Cheddi Jagan, is now a grudgingly accepted fact. The specifics—who, when, why, how often, how much—are not fully known. It was reported that Mr. Burnham's association with the CIA was so special that not even the U.S. ambassador in Georgetown knew about it. In like manner neither the Guyana ambassador in Washington nor the consul in Los Angeles knew anything about the Peoples Temple/Guyana government connection beyond what was necessary for routine consular business.

Perhaps the most disturbingly secret act of Mr. Burnham was when in 1966, at the same time the country became independent of Britain, he entered into a military agreement with the U.S. government, the terms of which some legal authorities claimed, surrendered the country's newly won territorial sovereignty. It was not until years later when the

A New Look at JONESTOWN

agreement became a public document in due process of U.S. affairs that the matter was made known in Guyana by the underground press.

In domestic affairs, the government's political acts, particularly those relating to elections, are said to be ten thousand times worse than Watergate.

A background as outlined here lends credence to the worst of expectations. But if for the moment that possibility is ruled out, could it be that the prime minister and government were just simply conned by a grand master of the art? After all, a few Americans have before conned the Guyana administration in some of the most hilarious rip-offs one can think of.

How Jones was able to mesmerize his followers could not work in dealing with a foreign government that had no need for the earthly paradise Jones envisioned. But Jones's ploys were big-time, none the less. Here are two examples:

1. He had printed in the Guyana state-owned press a photograph of himself with Vice President Mondale with a caption that he (Jones) was discussing aid for Guyana.

2. He dropped hints that First Lady Mrs. Rosalynn Carter was going to visit the commune.

Yet, merely to talk with a Temple member revealed that all was not well in the commune. They were too anxious to tell you they were happy, and Guyanese know too well how people in "open prison" behave.

One must remember too that in dealing with Burnham, Jones was not dealing with an ordinary man. Among third-world leaders, Burnham is rated the smartest (in the good sense of the word). He out-foxed the rest of the Caribbean leaders in securing Guyana as headquarters of CARIFTA (Caribbean Free Trade Association)—a home site which is the greatest obstacle to the proper functioning of the body. His genius for this kind of maneuver is acknowledged even by his enemies, who would grudgingly admit that to preside over a nation so tiny and a people so few is a waste of his talent.

In a few words, Jones could not have duped Burnham. Yet Jones got what he wanted: a sanctuary outside the ambit of U.S. law enforcement. At the same time, this arrangement did not block out benefits he was accustomed to receive from the U.S., for example, the Social Security checks of his followers.

The privilege didn't end there. In de facto terms Peoples Temple was exempt from Guyana's customs and immigration regulations and for all practical purposes operated as a separate territorial entity. "A state-within-a-state" is how Eusi Kwayana characterized it. The nervous neutrality of the Guyanese soldiers in the face of the air-strip murders is explained away in true Guyanese fashion: "we didn't want to intervene in the internal affairs of America." (I have heard it said too that the Guyanese government's reluctance to publicize the Jonestown events is due to the fact that it views them as an American affair—irrelevant to the political and economic interests of the Guyanese people.)

The government's claim that it was interested in the Peoples Temple because its cooperative philosophy was the same as the government's is not fully borne out. For instance, the land leased to the Temple was considered by residents as barren.

Absolutely nothing can grow there. If by superior fertilization methods you manage to make trees and plants grow they still would not bring forth fruit. And if the highest technology is used — at an unprofitable cost — you might get results but that would just last for a short while. Any agricultural project in that district was doomed to failure — a fact well known to the Guyana government, which had tried with a cassava mill and canning factory. This writer was in the area in March, 1978, and saw weeds healthily poised to overtake the mill. One resident even suggested that it might be a good idea to convert the mill into a church since there was none in the area. As to the canning operation, no fruit and vegetable was forthcoming and the operators — even to try out the plant — had to can trench water. Also, the government's cooperative agricultural group in the area was said to be producing about $ 240.00 worth of crops at a cost of $4,800.00. (These figures were quoted me by an official of the project.)

Against this backdrop, more than the glare of the NBC cameras, Jones's downfall was imminent. His moans "I am crushed, I am crushed" are particularly pitiful.

The most important thing to a prime minister like Burnham is his image. To mould one is an expensive and risky proposition. Through a treacherous and uncertain route characterized by precipices and ravines, Burnham has come to be regarded as a front-line black third-world revolutionary. Jones was everything anathema to that image — he was American, white and religious — everything to avoid like the plague. The question remains unanswered — what could possibly be the nature of the deal that would make Burnham risk his most precious political assets?

Postscript:
The above article was based on material I collected when I visited Jonestown in March, 1978, just before I left the country permanently for the United States. I completed it in Los Angeles, California, in a week or two after the November 18, 1978, horror.

On the same day I arrived in Jonestown in March, 1978, I tried to arrange a meeting with Jim Jones and made my way to the Temple's compound. Even from a distance I could clearly see George Santayana's warning writ large: "Those who forget the past are doomed to repeat it." The attendant at the guardhouse was reading *Night*, by concentration camp survivor Elie Wiesel—a surreal thing, in retrospect. I told him I was writing a book and wanted to interview Jim Jones. "No disciple is available to conduct you to meet the master," he said. He apologized and suggested that I leave the address where I was staying. I did so.

On the next day a delegation from the Temple came to the place I was staying to "fetch me to the master." By that time I had heard so much about the Temple from the people that lived nearby that I became literally scared for my life. My only wish was to get out of there as fast as possible. I made an excuse and avoided that meeting.

Soon after I returned to Georgetown, two ladies from the Temple visited me at Central High School, where I was Deputy Principal. One of them, the senior one, was Sharon Amos. I could see fear and foreboding in her eyes and mannerism. She wanted to know why I wanted to see Jim Jones and whether she could help. I told her that I once lived in San Francisco where the Temple was based and I followed its work in the community. I also showed her a recent clipping (critical of the Temple) from the *San Francisco Chronicle* that a friend sent me. She began to closely read the piece, evidently forgetting I was at work and just took some time off to meet with her.

I left for a few minutes rather than just stand there and watch her carefully read the article. When I came back I saw her trying to tear off a piece of the clipping, which she had neatly creased. She didn't seem embarrassed that I caught her in the act. Indeed, she looked like a programmed specimen bent on doing the master's bidding. There and then I knew without a doubt that the Temple was not what it seemed or pretended to be. I read subsequently that Sharon Amos in her flat in Georgetown slit her children's throats and then her own in unison with the mass suicide of her 900+ brethren in Jonestown.

I   *Members & Survivors*

II *Residents & Visitors*

III   *Analysts & Critics*   ✓

IV *Editor & Compiler*

V *Appendix & Miscellany*

Chapter 7

The Jonestown Plantation

Lear K. Matthews and George K. Danns

[One of the first scholarly responses to the Jonestown tragedy came from University of Guyana sociologists Drs. Lear Matthews and George K. Danns. Their paper "Communities and Development in Guyana: A Neglected Dimension in Nation Building" was published by the University of Guyana (1980, 94 pps).

This section is derived from that paper and has three parts. Part I is an assessment of community development from the perspective of that time (1970s). The intent is to provide a backdrop for the Jonestown community that imploded in 1978. Part II is a verbatim transcription of the section of the Danns/Matthews paper that focused on Jonestown. In Part III, the two sociologists give an updated rejoinder on the subject, more than 30 years after the tragedy. —E.K.]

Part I: How Communities Function in Guyana

The task of planning for and spearheading development efforts in the Third World is largely, and in some cases exclusively, the lot of the state in those countries. As a consequence of this "national responsibility" a holistic approach informs development plans, which are expected to provide blueprints for solving the social and economic ills of the society. Countries whose approach to development and nation building are socialist in orientation have a tendency to view the nation as one large community with one common fate and a common orientation. Such an ideology justifies the centralization of authority and decision-making within the state system "in the national interest." Consequently any developmental efforts undertaken must be initiated by the state or, at least, sanctioned by it. In one-party states or dominant one-party systems such effort must also have the approval of watch-dog party institutions. The peoples in such countries are soon conditioned, expected or made to rely on the state and/or the party to mobilize and direct their efforts. Such a trend may be further reinforced by an inherited dependency syndrome, a pattern of non-self-reliance brought about by colonizing powers. In a "planned change approach" adopted by such countries, the "nation's interests" and "national development" is posited as paramount and the notion of community development is ignored or else de-emphasized.

Guyana is one such socialist oriented third-world nation in which community development is submerged in a planned change process where communities are not to be seen as distinct from the nation and consequently there is no concept of "community development" as separate from "national development." National development is community development, and nation is seen as the community to be developed.

One of the Guyana government's leading showpieces was Melanie Damishana, a government-promoted community. It was referred to as a patronage community, and one of the projects passed off as manifestation of community development.

The price of such communities to residents is unquestioned loyalty and political support for the governing regime.

Government-sponsored groups such as Cuffy Farmers' Cooperative Society and the Youth Corps were at the forefront of these early attempts at pioneer resettlement development. The settlements included those at Matthews Ridge, Moco-Moco, Marudi, New River, and the more recent Linden/Soesdyke Highway Projects (Kuru Kururu), Yarowkabra, Long Creek, Dora, Clemwood, and Moblissa). Those on the Linden/Soesdyke settlements have attained some of the outlined objectives.

Gordon Payne (Payne, 1977), in his survey of settlements in Guyana, made a useful comparison between those in the Matthews Ridge area who had come from abroad and those who had resided only in Guyana (1976). Payne pointed out that most of the settlers had been "wage earners" and the attempt to make them farming settlers was problematic. It was found that most of the settlers preferred to establish and maintain individual farms rather than working in land cooperatives. To a great extent, community self-reliance and self-sufficiency are planned, supervised, and implemented—if not initiated—by the state. Furthermore, planned national implementation of community programs turns out to be systems of political patronage.

Community-inspired self-reliance efforts are stifled and precluded by various structural barriers, and social atrophy pervades the communities. People are losing any meaningful concept of community or relationships as the community interests are sacrificed to the "national interest." There is no adequate building of communities or committed community involvement. This lack of "community" is partly attributed to a state system in which structural confusion and functional obscurity associated with conflicting lines of authority characterize activities within and between state institutions. For example, there are many instances where it is not clear which government ministry performs what function.

Our position in this paper is that national development can only come about through community development. A nation is not a nation without communities and, therefore, to develop communities is to develop the nation. If communities are developed, so is the nation. Communities should be given greater decisional autonomy in their developmental efforts. State involvement should take the form of giving encouragement, guidelines and assistance rather than for the purpose of total direction and control. A philosophy of self-reliance and the cooperative as a vehicle of societal transformation can only be realized through community autonomy. However the present arrangement does not permit this. Instead, communication and direction for action stems from top down. This seems to suggest an attitude of disrespect on the part of the state for the people insofar as they are treated as if they are not capable of promoting their own change and development. As a result, the continuous inputs of control by the state into the very life of the communities retards rather than promotes self-reliance.

Part II: Life in Jonestown

Determined to implement its hinterland expansion program and desirous of counteracting failures as well as overcoming Guyanese resistance to resettlement, the government of Guyana offered resources and encouragement for hinterland development, including in its policy the invitation to foreigners to settle in the interior. Given this policy of encouraging foreign settlers, a group of Americans under a controversial character named Jim Jones took up settlement in the interior. This settlement, named Jonestown by Guyanese officials after its founder, was undoubtedly the largest and most advanced foreign community in Guyana. Though virtually unknown to most Guyanese, the Jonestown community and its development was evidently entrenched within the government's development plans.

Jonestown, also known as Peoples Temple Agricultural Project, was to be a model experiment in community development and was expected "to provide a community where new methods of food production and crops could be tried and made available to others in the developing country of Guyana" (Jonestown Booklet). To this end more than 3,000 (other estimates say 4,000) acres of interior land were allocated to the project in 1974 and many valuable in-kind services were offered. The community of foreign settlers was further given the government's blessing and sponsorship as a model settlement, exemplifying the type of community activity that would be instrumental in the transition to cooperative socialism. The interest here is not to examine the Jonestown that died or the events which led to its final tragic destruction, but more importantly to analyze the Jonestown settlement that existed as a community development project in Guyana.

It is clear that Jonestown was an experiment in human organization involving migrating people searching for a "better life," which objective was encouraged by officials of a state struggling to conquer the problems of underdevelopment.

If indeed autonomous development requires the development of an indigenous technology which would protect its self-reliance, then the continuance of imported technology will prolong dependence. This is a principle with which governments of third-world countries are well aware. Although the intent of the government of Guyana was to use Jonestown as a model in local community development, the utilization of indigenous resources as is normally encouraged was not part of the practice at Jonestown. Herein lies a contradiction in policy as it relates to hinterland resettlements in Guyana.

Jonestown was a "transplanted" community and as far as is known consisted mainly of American citizens. It had its own infrastructure and imported foreign technology. Medical facilities, communications systems, and even a substantial portion of the community's rations were transported from the United States. Although it had the capacity to produce in abundance, one is left to wonder how self-sufficient Jonestown really was.

The development of indigenous resources is also intricately interwoven into the scheme for national development and projects such as Jonestown are viewed as expeditious attempts to promote nation building. The overall goal of the Jonestown community was to benefit Guyanese through effort of expanding and improving cultivation and the eventual development of Guyana's interior. But this transplanted community was a sponsored creation and had a relationship with the government based on political patronage. This community received patronage benefits from the government in return for their intimate involvement in carrying programs of the ruling PNC party. In particular it seemed that "diplomatic" immunity and special privileges were exchanged for political favors.

Furthermore, Jonestown residents were given special treatment and incentives by the government, including tax-free privileges and special radio time to promote their "development activities." In times when Guyana was experiencing shortages of certain basic commodities caused partly by foreign exchange restrictions, residents of Jonestown, a community thus named by Guyanese officials, had access to resources which were restricted from distribution to Guyanese. The community was also immune from any sort of customs tariff and police regulation; and equipment including weapons were transferred without any scrutiny by Guyanese officials. This enabled the Jonestown residents to build a settlement with modern facilities in the jungles of Guyana.

The settlement was provided with most of its facilities from abroad. In a sense, for the American citizens, Jonestown represented not only an alternative to the "hardships" they had experienced at home in the United States, but, it was meant to be a home away from home since Jim Jones the group leader provided some facilities of the material life to which they were accustomed. Particularly impressive was the medical services, which responded adequately to almost any ailment that members of the community may have encountered. In the medical clinic, which was well stocked and prepared to give first aid at all times, the primary focus was preventive medicine. It is important to point out that no other community in Guyana is equipped to carry out such services.

In order to understand the structure and function of the Peoples Temple Agricultural Project, we have developed a model to analyze the real Jonestown, an approach that puts into perspective the hidden dimension of this unique planned change effort. The community itself had a seemingly comprehensive and progressive social and economic program. Through such a program the hope was to build and sustain a very unique socialist community in a society whose dominant ideology was cooperative socialism. However, upon closer examination of the real objectives or intentions of the Peoples Temple leader Jim Jones and his relationship with others of the Jonestown community, one would see a modern-day slavery plantation.

Jonestown was an atavism, a recreation of a slave plantation with similar characteristics. First of all the relationship between Jim Jones and the mass of Jonestown residents was one of a master/slave relationship. The master and his white lieutenants came to Guyana similar to the transatlantic journeying of earlier white colonizers. Secondly, the majority of the population who were brought to Guyana and who comprised the bulk of the labor force were African Americans and were also brought under slave-like conditions. For instance, they went through a process of dehumanization in which they were required to give up all their possessions, were cut off from contact with their families and country of origin and made to sublimate their passions and orient their behavior in accordance with the austere demands of the dominant Jim Jones. All of this was very similar to what slaves who were brought to work the plantations four centuries earlier endured. Stripped of their identity and dragged out of their homes, they were forced to become tools of production. The community of Jonestown residents, like the slaves on the plantations, did not own anything except their individual labor power.

Religion had a similar function in both institutions. Whereas under the colonial plantation system religion was used as a tool of conversion to total obedience and docility, in the case of the Peoples Temple it was used to lure people to join the organization. Religion in this atavistic community could be viewed as a device for preliminary indoctrination, conversion and control, which were sustained by harsh discipline reminiscent of the earlier plantation experience.

Jonestown was a total institution with a closed system with the productive and social features comparable to the plantation milieu. The total lives of the residents were carefully scheduled with only the trusted lieutenants or "house slaves" and "slave drivers" allowed to communicate with the outside. There was a social hierarchy in which Jones and other whites were at the top of the stratification system. This points to a similar situation within the hierarchical arrangements of colonial plantation in which white superiority was pronounced.

There was perpetual fear among the residents of Jonestown. Just as how on the slave plantation harsh punishment including flogging was meted out for disobedience, so among the residents, disobedient members were punished. As one member stated: "A rule breaker might have his head shaved or be forced to wear a yellow hard hat as a badge of dishonor or told not to speak for several days. If clothing or tools were damaged or lost … the member would be denied his meals …." (Kilduff, 1978, p. 89). Furthermore, Jonestown members were fearful of being caught and punished if they attempted to escape. Similarly, runaway slaves were in constant fear of being tracked down and punished.

The housing of the residents of Jonestown was reminiscent of the colonial plantation housing. There were uncomfortable, overcrowded shacks. Like slaves, the Jonestown members were compelled to work long hours—from 7.00 a.m. to 6.00 p.m. on week days and from 7.00 a.m. to 2.00 p.m. on Sundays—with very little rest. Almost every meal comprised of rice and gravy (Kilduff, 1978, p. 118).

Jonestown residents, unlike plantation slaves who had no hope of "freedom" and promised very little for life in the future, were expecting a utopia—a place free from the prejudices and other social ills experienced in the United States. This situation was similar to that of indentured laborers who were promised land and a passage back to their native land as well as to that of slaves who were encouraged to develop "other worldly" expectations.

This recreated sponsored community was then intended from the government's perspective to represent another strategy for decolonization and development. But instead, it turned out to be a suppressed community with a fascistic political organization.

To finalize this section, we will compare the Jonestown community with the local communities.

Jonestown as far as we know had minimum interference from the Guyanese government, enjoyed autonomy as no other foreign or Guyanese community did and flourished in its material developments.

Because of the significance of Jonestown to Guyana in view of the government's development plans and because it was indeed viewed as a community development project, our analysis extends to an important comparison between the Jonestown community and local Guyanese communities.

Jonestown, like all of the other "created communities" in Guyana was not really self-sufficient. Much of its supplies, including rations were imported. There was also a heavy reliance on foreign technology, not unlike many local communities.

Jonestown residents were not really concerned with the development of the country but with the development of their own microcosmic world. In the case of the local communities, although the government expects the people to be interested in national development, the concern is realistically development of one's immediate surroundings.

There were some very important differences between the two types of communities. First of all the people at Jonestown were non-Guyanese with a different culture and different work ethic. This suggests that whether or not they were governed by strict compliance norms, there would have been dedication and commitment to such an effort. Most of the Jonestown residents were people with problems seeking a utopian existence which they hoped would be eventually realized at Jonestown. Members of local communities are more concerned with eking out a better living by contributing to incremental improvement of their families and communities.

Jonestown, in addition, was more than a community. It was a cult, a community of obedience and compulsion in which cult members were largely coerced and constrained. The local communities were more voluntary, and the government could intervene as often as it desired to do so. Jonestown was more autonomous, with Jim Jones the central authority. What started out as a utopian experiment in community building ended up as a nightmare of disaster for its residents.

Part III: Jonestown – reflections 35 years after

On this the 36th anniversary of the Peoples Temple tragedy in Guyana, we reflect on dimensions of that unconscionable disaster. The story of the Peoples Temple symbolizes (a) the fallibility of persons whose path to the "American dream" has been frustrated because of economic hardship, political ideology or their ethnicity and (b) developing nations' vulnerability to sundry international influences as they struggle to stymie conditions of poverty. The choices made by victims of discrimination and injustice vary from complacency to desperate group action, the latter characterizing the genesis of Jonestown.

This unprecedented event on November 18, 1978, in which more than 900 lives were lost, occurred after members of a religious cult settlement drank cyanide-laced Kool-Aid. *[The drink was actually Flavor-Aid, a British version of Kool-Aid. —E.K]*

Reportedly a significant number of the dead were African Americans, and about a third of them children. Led by a controversial religious character, Jim Jones, it is believed that some of the members were shot as they attempted to escape. *[This was from an early report but only 2 members were verified to have died from gunshots, one of whom was Jim Jones himself. —E.K.]*

Lest we forget, that event set off an international fervor, eliciting conversations about cults, the role of religion and politics in violence, terrorism and racism. There have been lingering questions about the surreptitious nature of Jonestown and benefits incurred by officials from Guyana and the United States. Unfortunately, the tragedy was for many North Americans their "introduction" to the nation of Guyana and the erroneous belief that the majority of those directly involved were native Guyanese. This rejoinder examines the nature of a community development project gone awry and the psycho-social impact on marginalized people. The actions of a megalomaniac, group dependency and experimentation in nation building characterized the Jonestown experience. It was the brainchild of an idealistic foreigner, who was initially supported by officials in the United States, and encouraged by the ideals of post-colonial nation building.

Virtually unknown to most Guyanese, Jonestown became the largest and most advanced immigrant community in Guyana. It is believed that the group was given free reins to the interior because of the Guyana-Venezuela border dispute. Jonestown provided an American presence that Venezuela presumably dared not penetrate. This surrealistic community was viewed, given the government's blessing as a prototype settlement, as representing the sort of activity instrumental in the transition to "cooperative socialism." In retrospect, it was doomed to failure. Not only were the CIA and American embassy more informed about Peoples Temple than were local military officials, but the latter were ostensibly prevented from investigating that "isolated community" until after the tragedy.

Jones misled his followers by promising to take care of their basic needs. It was an experiment in human organization, involving a people searching for a better life and enticed by officials of a state struggling to conquer the problems of underdevelopment. Many members believed that they could create a community free from the problems encountered at home. Although this north-south migration deviated from contemporary immigration patterns, like immigrants today, participants were after an elusive "dream."

Religion was used for preliminary indoctrination, conversion and control, sustained by harsh discipline reminiscent of the slave plantation centuries earlier. Duped by the performances of staged faith healing events, followers, as well as officials in the U.S. and Guyana, were manipulated into believing the authenticity of Jones's project. Not only were members encouraged to develop other worldly expectations, but to expect a utopia—a place free from the prejudices and other social ills in the United States. Held against their will, some of the residents suffered from mental distress due to the reported confining and regimented structure of the community, while Jones displayed clear symptoms of anxiety and paranoia in the days leading up to the disaster.

The Peoples Temple debacle emerged from three divergent motivations: the Jonestown residents' desire to create a better world, the Guyana government's plan to develop the interior, and Jones's determination to re-establish a power base away from U.S. soil. What started out as a utopian experiment in community building ended up an improbable venture, embarrassing to unsuspecting Guyanese, and a deadly alternative for hundreds of disenchanted Americans, who are often blamed for their own victimization. Ironically, a recent proposal to make Jonestown a tourist attraction can be viewed as an attempt to capitalize on an unprecedented, transnational man-made disaster and submitting to human curiosity.

More than thirty years later, there have been worldwide movements such as the Arab spring and the Wall Street Movement, seeking alternatives, desperately embracing democratic values and changes. The government of Guyana has entered hinterland development agreements with foreign states such as China. Although such contracts have the potential for exploitation of the country's resources and create challenges for its sovereignty, the consequences should benefit the nation as a whole. Hopefully, similar tragedies will not be repeated. We shall never forget, but must thrive to overcome our differences as an ingredient for social justice and sustainability.

Chapter 8

Context for Leo Ryan's Involvement with Jonestown

James P. Garrett

Background

I will try to summarize the social and historical context of the times that Congressman Leo Ryan was active in. It is important to understand the social and historical context in which he emerged as a progressive congressman and the inter-locking forces and conditions which led Ryan to travel to Jonestown, Guyana, on November 18, 1978, where he was killed by orders from Reverend Jim Jones.

The political situation of those times reflected a transition from broad-based, intensely militant form of struggle all over the U.S. (anti-racist, anti-war, anti-government) and a hands-on 1960s style of progressive politics to a less militant, localized Democratic Party-directed and spiritually centered form of involvement in the 1970s. Leo Ryan developed his political skills and prominence during this period of expansion and contraction and was certainly shaped by the times. He was also greatly affected by his association with key people (Willie Brown, Jesse Unruh, and Angela Davis) and organizations

(Black Panther Party, Glide Memorial Church, and a roundtable of leading San Francisco Democratic Party figures) that played historic roles in those times.

By 1976-1978, with the internal collapse/state-fostered liquidation of the Black Panther Party (BPP) and other radical political organizations, it was clear that the goal of militant socialist revolution had failed. The dispersal, incarceration or assassination of the remnants of progressive forces led by COINTELPRO (Counter Intelligence Program), the constant pressure from external forces (police agencies, collapse of U.S. global economic hegemony/recession, transition to a post-colonial world), the explosion of internal contradictions (personal corruption, drug addition, Post-Traumatic Stress Disorder [PTSD], opportunism, collective frenzy for individual place, peace, and escape from social norms) were symptoms of a general malaise and loss of purpose widespread in leftist communities in the Bay Area. During this period Leo Ryan came into prominence as an elected congressman. At the same time, Jim Jones rose to even greater prominence as a minister of the social gospel and a leader of what was left of progressive political organization in the Bay Area. All of these historic forces connected. The dynamics that produced Jim Jones and Leo Ryan converged tragically in Jonestown, Guyana, South America. So let us go back.

Bay Area Activism
Leo Ryan, as was the case of Jim Jones, was born and raised in the Midwest. Ryan was born and raised in Nebraska. Jones hails from Indiana. After service in World War II, Ryan migrated to California and settled in South San Francisco, where from 1956 to 1962 he was a high school teacher and band director.

Leo Ryan found his place within the dominant liberal consensus of the time, one that proscribed to the general acceptance of U.S. hegemony over the world in the era after WWII. Under the umbrella of U.S. world dominance, many young people (particularly young white men raised in the Catholic Church to believe that good works may trump mea culpa) sought avenues to provide service to those whose lives needed amelioration while preparing to accept opportunity for personal advancement whenever it arose. Ryan like many others was raised to live in a culture where there would be no reason to expect earthly tragedy or despair. The Bay Area, with its rapid growth and general prosperity, was an excellent setting for both service and opportunity. (For further details, refer to *City for Sale: The Transformation of San Francisco* [Hartman, 2002].)

By 1961, Leo Ryan was already active in Democratic Party politics in South San Francisco, a rapidly growing suburb of San Francisco. In that year, he attended President Kennedy's inauguration, and in his own words became "inspired to a life in public service." The Democratic Party remained the consistent and reliable channel for Ryan to manifest his inspiration.

During the decade of John Kennedy's inauguration and Leo Ryan's inspiration, the Bay Area became a center of progressive and radical political/social movements. This was characterized by the rise and fall of a number of radicalized groups. At UC Berkeley, for example, a few black students (less than 70 were enrolled at Berkeley in 1961, and most of those were on athletic scholarship) in league with several off campus black activist groups formed the Afro-American Association (AAA). Over the next five years AAA used the readings of Marcus Garvey, the recordings of Malcolm X and the realities of racism faced on the Berkeley Campus and the surrounding cities, especially Oakland to build black intellectual leadership that was both nationalist and progressive. The AAA meshed ideologies of racial pride and unity with demands for radical economic change. The AAA produced or affected future leaders as Melvin and Huey Newton, Bobby Seale, Hon. Ronald Dellums, Ron Everett (Maulana Karenga), Willie Brown, and international activists like Donald Warden and Tchaiko Kwayana. (For further details refer to *The Black Power Movement: Rethinking the Civil Rights-Black Power Era* [Joseph: 2006] and *Waiting 'Til the Midnight Hour* [Joseph: 2006].)

During the same period, San Francisco became the locus for the growth of white-radical and -led labor and student activism. Initially disparate, this growing movement consolidated in 1960, with the Anti-HUAC demonstrations that took place at the San Francisco City Hall where several hundred students and labor leaders were arrested. This activism expanded from 1962-64 with the Auto-Row and Mel's Drive-in demonstrations that challenged the refusal of local businesses to hire blacks for other than menial jobs. Drawing heavily on the southern Civil Rights Movement, this mainly white student-led (though labor funded and communist party influenced) activism drew many students from San Francisco State College and later from UC Berkeley.

By 1964-66, many Bay Area social activists joined the Democratic Party. They established caucuses within the party to force it to open elective offices to progressives and minorities. These efforts resulted in the consolidation of a strong liberal wing of the Democratic Party in the Bay Area. Leo Ryan was an excited participant in these developments.

John and Phil Burton, Willie Brown (under the tutelage of Jesse Unruh, whom he later replaced as Speaker of the State Assembly), and Ronald Dellums were among those who were elected to state offices during this period. Leo Ryan, active as early as 1960 in the Kennedy wing of the Democratic Party, was elected Mayor of South San Francisco in 1962. After serving as Mayor for less than a year, he was elected to the California State Assembly where he served for 10 years. (*Leo Ryan: Official Congressional Biography, Congressional Record 1978.*)

Ideologies for All

However, during this period, militant activism remained at the forefront. At the time a broad spectrum of political thought germinated in the Bay Area. Leftist political ideologies ranged from Maoist communist groups (Progressive Labor), to the establishment (Soviet Union-supported) Communist Party USA, the Trotskyite Socialist Workers Party, and the social democratic SDS. Radical black nationalist and political ideologies expanded beyond the confines of the local black communities and joined the debates. Contentious debates between these ideologically disparate groups and forces were rampant both outside of and within Democratic Party organizations in the Bay Area.

A rapidly growing counter culture (called Hippie) movement emerged in the San Francisco Haight-Ashbury District (lodged in between Kezar Stadium and Golden Gate Park). Similar anti-establishment tendencies also developed around the campuses of the University of California at Berkeley and at San Francisco State College. Those who joined the Hippie movement (mainly young and white), though not overtly political, usually adopted a range of liberal views on use of drugs, sexual freedom, Southern black civil rights activism, gay and lesbian rights, and freedom of movement on the streets. Distinctive and colorful clothing were a mark of distinction for the culture of grey conformity that the hippies were trying to escape. The Hippies' contribution to the rock and folk music explosion in the Bay Area and beyond may have been its most enduring cultural contribution. Several rock bands that developed in the Haight-Ashbury music scene during the 1960s became famous and toured internationally (Grateful Dead, Big Brother and the Holding Company, Jefferson Airplane, later Jefferson Starship).

Many Hippies were strongly opposed to the Vietnam War. Thousands of Hippies participated in mass rallies and demonstrations that were held almost weekly in San Francisco or Berkeley.

Between 1966 and 1972, black community militancy and rebellion led struggles around the U.S. generally and in the Bay Area particularly. Urban uprisings took place in Detroit, Cleveland, Chicago, and in San Francisco's Hunters Point. Black workers gained status in an increasingly militant labor movement just as U.S. based manufacturing peaked and began a steep decline. Anti-war activism dominated most campuses. Black Student Unions (BSU), formed on predominantly white college campuses, filtered downward into high schools and middle schools. The first and strongest of the BSUs, based at San Francisco State College, developed a Black Studies Curriculum with the goal of introducing the black experience at the college level. The battle for its inclusion in the college curriculum led to the longest student-led strike in U.S. history (with strong support from faculty, the city's teachers, the longshoremen workers union (ILWU), broad sectors of the

SF/Bay Area black community, and the liberal wing of the Democratic Party).

Black Panthers
In1966, two separate Black Panther parties were formed, one in San Francisco, the other in Oakland (Lewis, n.d.). The leaders of both BPPs were former members of the AAA. The Black Panther title was taken from the symbol for the Lowndes County Alabama Freedom Organizations (LCFO). Organized by an all-black contingent of members of the Student Non-Violent Coordinating Committee (SNCC) led by Stokeley Carmichael, LCFO incorporated the now famous call for "Black Power" to stress aggressive black militant leadership. Black Panther, Black Power, and slogans such as "Move on Over, or We'll Move on Over You," expressed major challenges to the non-violent, integrationist leadership of the southern Civil Rights Movement and its slogan "We Shall Overcome." The shift to all-black organizing by SNCC came in the wake of the failure to seat the SNCC-led Mississippi Freedom Democratic Party at the 1964 National Democratic Convention in Atlantic City, New Jersey. (In addition to the Peniel Joseph's books mentioned, see also *Bloody Lowndes: Civil Rights and Black Power in Alabama's Black Belt* [Jeffries, 2009].)

The Bay Area BPPs were openly militant. They were also politically radical, calling for black community self determination, anti-imperialism (especially in support of Cuba, Vietnam, and South Africa), and anti-capitalism (restructuring the US economy to benefit minorities and the poor). In a short time the Oakland-based Black Panther Party for Self-Defence overwhelmed and crushed the San Francisco BPP. With Huey Newton and Bobby Seale as its initial leaders, its "guns in front" militancy drew to its ranks hundreds of young blacks and chapters spread quickly to nearly 25 cities and towns in the U.S. The BPP and the Peace and Freedom Party (PFP) coalition, tumultuous as it was, remained viable into the 1970s.

In 1968 the BPP, with its exponential visibility and notoriety, united with progressive whites (termed by Eldridge Cleaver as "mother country radicals" Peace and Freedom Party/Yippies) to challenge California and National liberal Democrats at the Democratic Party Convention in Chicago on its domestic and international policy. Leo Ryan served as a delegate to the 1964 convention and was very prominent in the tumultuous 1968 Convention. It was later noted by Jackie Speier (who traveled to Guyana with Ryan) that Ryan had vacillated between supporting the candidacies of Eugene McCarthy and Robert Kennedy.

Initial Gains

Among the programs greatly affected by radical atmosphere that was rampant in the Bay Area was the Prison Visitation Program. Initially the program allowed both family and non-family visitations and was sponsored by the California Corrections and Rehabilitation System. Over time it blossomed into co-education and cultural activities (plays, Chorals, classes in political education, modern dance and in some situations, clandestine love affairs). Gang members and criminals, absorbed by either the ideologies and/or rhetoric from radical teachings in political education classes conducted by white and black radicals and by the obvious mass uprisings that were taking place in their own neighborhoods, became politically conscious, vocal advocates of prison reform, and in some cases, revolution. (See *The Rise and Fall of California's Radical Prison Movement* [Cummins, 1994].)

In 1970, Assemblyman Leo Ryan became so caught up in the prison reform effort, that, using a pseudonym, he got himself arrested, strip-searched and funneled through the California prison system. Ryan ended up spending 10 days in the notorious Folsom Prison (remember Johnny Cash's "Folsom Prison Blues") while presiding as chairman of the Prison Reform Oversight Committee for the California State Assembly.

By 1972, the visitation program had been transformed into the beginnings of a Prison Reform Movement. The Radical Prison Movement, with its in-house spokespeople (e.g., George Jackson) and public leaders (e.g., Angela Davis) became a very important issue for social and religious activists and politicians at the time. The idea of public witness, so important in the Martin Luther King's social gospel and Civil Rights movement, led to increasing empathy with the plight of convicted felons (Cummins, 1994).

Blowback
Blowback by various government forces in California and at the federal level began immediately and expanded with increasing ferocity over time. In 1968, Ronald Reagan, the governor of California, declared war on "Communists, the Black Panther Party and the Hippie counter-culture."

Richard Nixon and Governor Reagan joined at the hip on these shared goals.

The U.S. Justice Department and the FBI provided financial and training resources to support local law enforcement efforts. Local police and state law enforcement and prison guard agencies designed and implemented programs to infiltrate, neutralize and destroy progressive organizations and individuals of all strata. Within a short time police forces were militarized in training equipment and tactics. Mass demonstrations, which in the past had been tolerated by San Francisco Police, were summarily attacked. Hundreds of demonstrators were beaten and arrested. Pitched battles were waged between police and demonstrators around the Bay Area and across the country. The violent blowback was exhibited blatantly in 1968 during the four-month long black student-led and faculty-supported student strike at San Francisco State College. Students and citizens who joined picket lines and rallies to legitimize ethnic studies courses on the campus were attacked and beaten almost daily by local and state police officers.

The FBI established the Counter-Intelligence Program (COINTELPRO) and Special Operations 12 (SO12) for the purpose of carrying out more sophisticated programs of the infiltration, disruption and liquidation of activist individuals and groups. *[Originally COINTELPRO was formed in 1956 as a covert operation against the Communist Party of the USA. —E.K.]* During the next seven years militant groups like the BPP, Black Students Union, and Students for a Democratic Society were targeted, their leaderships were divided, entrapped, isolated (in the case of the Panthers, several key leaders were assassinated with the assistance of COINTELPRO), their ranks depleted by imprisonment and exile. Across the U.S., many activist organizations targeted by the FBI and/or its local progeny, were destroyed by infiltration and/or internal disarray.

The Radical Prison Movement was upended by two major forces: The first was the politicization of Prison Guards into an anti-reform group. They fought to kill all reform efforts to be substituted by higher wages for the guards and draconian punishment for those who were prisoners. Secondly there was the problem of a lack of a strong political cohesion within the prison movement itself. There was no formal organization to absorb released prisoners. And usually no means of support other than criminal activity was possible. Once released, some became attached to local organizations. Without continuing exposure to organized political development, many former convicts fell back into the life style they adopted that led to their incarceration. This may have also included individuals who adopted the trappings of political rhetoric and style picked up from the Radical Prison Movement. One example was the Symbianese Liberation Army. In 1975, this group, led by a former member of the movement, kidnapped socialite student Patty Hearst and assassinated a popular black Bay Area public school official under a banner of leading "The Socialist Revolution." The SLA also engaged in a number of bank robberies and shootings before most of their members were burned to death in a fire set by the Los Angeles Police (Cummins, 1994).

The counter-culture communities in Berkeley and San Francisco were also infiltrated with police agents, drugs and violence. While the ideals of an open community remained intact, its reality was being sabotaged by provocateurs, heroin traffickers, robbery, and extortionists. Law enforcement agencies aided and abetted in its decimation. At the same time an impending global financial crisis with the collapse of the U.S. post-war economic domination would starve the Hippie community of its financial base.

The unraveling and dismantling of dozens of counter-culture communes in the Bay Area and around the U.S. coincided with the end of the Vietnam War. Police raids against visible community leaders and institutions (free clinics, marijuana dispensaries, rape crisis centers, flop houses) weakened the counter-culture to its foundation. Shortly after the Vietnam War ended in 1975, young white males who had avoided the draft were allowed to return home or move about without legal punishment. Thousands of young women also returned to home or college or settled in to marriage both within and outside the communes.

The Counter-Culture of the 60s

As more militant activist groups were being attacked, many people on the left retreated from all involvement. Fear and distrust quickly replaced unity and joint action. There were instances of organization leaders and members of rank and file turning on each other often with tragic results.

Although there were many examples of dissolution or decimation of militant organizations, especially by 1975, progressive and liberal projects continued. The "Social Gospel," churches, and community redevelopment efforts and the Democratic Party began to replace radical organizations as a base for progressive activities in the Bay Area.

Church congregations, always a refuge in the wake of failed struggles by the black community movements, once again experienced a growth spurt. Churches that adopted "the Social Gospel," drawn in large part from the writings of Dr. Martin Luther King, was especially popular with remnants of the left without regard to color. Among the several churches with leaders who preached the social gospel that experienced increases in its congregation was Peoples Temple, whose minister was Jim Jones. Rev. Jones and some of his congregation were newly transferred from Indiana to Ukiah, California (where Jones prophesied Nuclear Conflagration), then to San Francisco. In San Francisco, Jones re-inaugurated Peoples Temple Church as a model for a future "Beloved Community." (See *Violence and Religious Commitment* ... [Levi, 1981].)

Membership also grew in Bay Area Democratic Party Clubs. The Democratic Party was considered to be relatively safe though its reputation for left wing collaboration was well known by local and national police forces. Leo Ryan, elected to Congress in 1973, was among the key members of the Democratic Party Leadership Round Table (LRT). The LRT, funded by corporate families like the Haas (Levis Jeans), directed many Bay Area civic and re-development projects. Although not as prominent as the Burtons and Willie Brown, Ryan increasingly became a leading spokesperson for liberal democratic policy and programs under the LRT. As a congressman, Ryan became well known for his strong support of expanding funds for education. He was also a strong critic of the CIA and of covert operations. He co-authored the Ryan-Hughes Amendment, which would have required extensive CIA notice to Congress prior to engaging in Covert Operations. Ryan was also well known for his criticism of cult-religions like L. Ron Hubbard's Scientology and Sun Myung Moon's Unification Church. (Also told in the PBS American Experience episode, *Jonestown: The Life and Death of Peoples Temple* [Nelson, 2006].)

During this same period, community based resistance to Urban Renewal efforts in San Francisco grew as it achieved greater access to the political process. Before World War II, the Fillmore historical district had a mixed Japanese/black population. With the incarceration of Japanese-Americans during the war, Fillmore's population became flush with black emigrants from the South. Black businesses and institutions replaced those left by the Japanese. Although in the post-war era several efforts at urban renewal and black removal were pursued, the results were mixed. Post-Kennedy era federal funding of over $100 million, along with renewed support from business interests, pushed the process forward (see Hartman).

In opposition to urban renewal stood the remnants of the Johnson/Kennedy era anti-poverty programs. These community based organizations survived at low operating levels but sustained trained local organizers on the payrolls. One such program was the Western Addition Political Action Committee (WAPAC), ostensibly organized to represent the local community in its opposition to efforts by local developers, construction craft unions and the U.S. federal government to transform and gentrify the Fillmore District.

Over a tumultuous 10-year period, WAPAC and its coalition of anti-poverty organizers, local politicians, government bureaucrats, radical ideologues, hustlers, ex-convicts, opportunists, police agents, student radicals, LGBT activists, and religious leaders led futile attempts, first to resist, then to moderate the evacuation of the black, artistic and counter-culture communities from Fillmore (Hartman).

Ryan and Jones Cross Paths

By the end of 1976 the Fillmore District redevelopment/gentrification conflict was at its height. Although WAPAC retained offices in the Fillmore, many of its mass meetings took place at Peoples Temple. Speakers at these rallies included noted radicals such as Angela Davis, leading Democrats Willie Brown, Harvey Milk, Leo Ryan, Dianne Feinstein and Jim Jones. Informal alliances with these established personalities consolidated support for WAPAC's resistance to gentrification and also addressed issues of police abuse, and cuts in social welfare programs (Hartman, 2002).

As was the case with most of the Bay Area Democratic Leadership, Ryan was initially very supportive of Jim Jones and his brand of Social Gospel. Although his Congressional District office was in South San Francisco, a number of Leo Ryan's constituents, with his encouragement, became members of the Peoples Temple, which was located 30 minutes away, in San Francisco's Fillmore District.

However, reports of cultism and abuse in the Temple began to circulate to democratic office holders from various sources. Most elected officials including Willie Brown and Ryan dismissed these rumors as disinformation by FBI informants. Ryan became more suspicious with the death of former Temple Member Bob Houston, the son of a close friend, whose mutilated body was found by the railroad track three days after he taped conversation with his ex-wife in which leaving the Temple was discussed (Reiterman and Jacobs, 1982).

Negative rumors persisted to the point where there were calls for investigations into the activities of the Temple. Jim Jones decided to exile himself and his Peoples Temple from the U.S. and to seek paradise in South America. And many members of the Temple, already alienated from the U.S. because of various acts of repression, were convinced that the opportunity to leave and find paradise somewhere else was a great thing. Others went along because they felt lost without the Temple and the messianic Jones. All of this was taking place in the context of an ongoing alliance between Jones, leaders of the

Democratic Party Leadership Roundtable, and prominent progressives. ("Jones Captivated SF's Liberal Elite," *SFGate*, Nov. 12, 1998. Michael Taylor)

Relocation to Guyana and Aftermath

After the Temple moved to Jonestown, Guyana, in 1978, transporting more than 1,000 members, reports of direct violations of human rights, including torture surfaced. A body called Concerned Relatives Group was formed to petition in behalf of any member who wished to leave Jonestown, which was being constructed as an agricultural commune, to return to the U.S. Some of the members of the Concerned Relatives Group were Ryan's constituents and they appealed directly for his support. A negative article published in the San Francisco Examiner pushed him further.

For Congressman Leo Ryan, given his long history of opposition to cult religions, steeped in the Social Gospel ideal of public witness, and the fact that several of his constituencies were directly affected, it may have seemed reasonable for him to take a decision, fatefully, to go to Jonestown. He wanted to see the conditions in Jonestown for himself, and he felt it was his duty, to personally see to the release and return to the U.S. of any disaffected Temple members. Willie Brown, President Jimmy Carter, and a number of other prominent Democrats advised against the trip for safety and political reasons. The Prime Minister of Guyana, Forbes Burnham, was a friend to the National Democratic Party, whose leaders saw no crisis that required the presence of a very visible and now very prominent congressman.

Congressman Ryan apparently displayed no visible signs of fear. He and his staff planned the trip as well as could be expected. He was to travel to Guyana as part of a government investigation, funded by the U.S. government. Ryan made the trip formally as the chairman of a congressional subcommittee with jurisdiction over U.S. citizens living in a foreign country. He invited other members of the Bay Area congressional delegation to join him, but all refused. However, news of the trip hit the U.S. media and the trip became a major media event. By the date of departure, November 14, 1978, more than 30 people, including Ryan, Jackie Speier (survivor and future member of Congress), and several other members of his staff, 17 relatives or members of the Concerned Relatives Group, a number of news reporters and an NBC TV team were on the plane (Reiterman and Jacobs, 1982).

The rest is history.

Chapter 9

Jonestown: A Caribbean/Guyanese Perspective

Text of a talk given in 1979 at Stanford University

Walter Rodney

[The objective of this transcription is to maintain the character of the moment by leaving in those word forms that are normal when speaking to a live audience, even though they may be unnecessary and distracting—or even redundant—when put on paper.

Transcribing this particular event was made less easy because the talks, more or less, were given extemporaneously. Additionally, in the playback of the recording, some words were inaudible or undecipherable due to the quality of the recording.

When a word cannot be understood, and I am unable to make a reasonable guess, I have left it out and indicate the omission with an ellipsis (...). More serious incomprehension is labeled as "unintelligible" in parenthesis. Additionally, for the sake of clarity, I have in a few instances added a word or two, and these are indicated in square brackets

All in all, this transcript is as verbatim as readability allows. —E.K.]

Introduction by Dr. Ewart Thomas

... some of you, I am sure, know him from the classic text, *How Europe Underdeveloped Africa*, which provides to my mind a correct historical evaluation of the underdevelopment of Africa, and shows why development in Africa is not possible unless and until there is a radical break with the national capitalist system.

Some of you are also probably familiar with his definitive work on the Atlantic slave trade entitled *A History of the Upper Guinea Coast 1545 - 1800*. If you read it, [you will agree] it is a comprehensive examination from a radical perspective that debunks the myth some historians hold ... . Rodney shows convincingly that there was the existence of an export market that created the possibilities of the many forms of domestic slavery that were observed.

And a few of you might remember the shortest of his books called *The Groundings with my Brothers*, which happens to be my favorite book for a number of reasons. It is a living testimony of how the black intellectual can move beyond his or her own discipline and challenge the social niche that is invariably structured in a Eurocentric way. This short and brief book also shows how the black academic can develop his or her ideas in a positive way by attaching himself or herself to the activities of the black masses.

But then I personally remember him from high school, on the cricket field, as being a fearsome fast bowler, with a very long run-up. But he wasn't all that fast, it was the unpredictability of his direction [laughing]. It had opposing batsmen fearful for their lives. So there are a lot of reasons why we were very grateful when Rodney chose history, rather than ... [laughing].

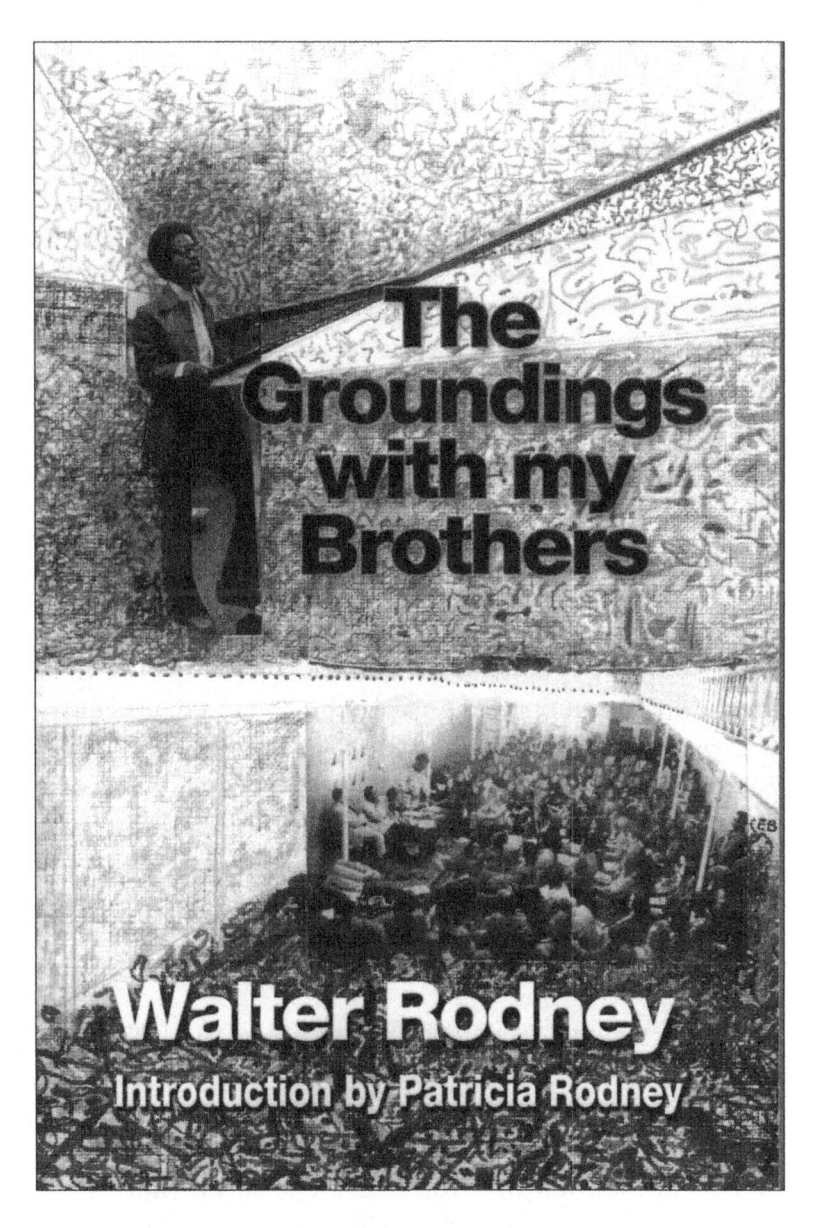

The most recent edition of *Groundings* with an introduction by Patricia Rodney. Walter Rodney Press, LLC, East Point, Georgia, USA. 2014.

He was born in Guyana in, in [pause] not that long ago [laughing]. He graduated from the University of the West Indies in Jamaica in 1963 with first class honors in history. Then he proceeded to the School of Oriental and African Studies at the University of London, where [at age 24] he finished the Ph.D. on the slave trade (his thesis was developed into the book referred to earlier). That thesis was written in 1966. From there he proceeded to Tanzania to teach at Dar es Salaam. Then he returned to Jamaica to teach at the University of the West Indies. That was about nine months before he was, as they say, refused entry after leaving the country for a short stay in Canada. And this [Jamaican government declaring Dr. Rodney persona non grata], to my mind, ... historians will regard as a watershed in recent Caribbean history.

There were popular demonstrations in support of the work that Walter was doing in Jamaica before he was denied entry. And many of the movements we saw in the late 60s and early 70s are closely tied to the event of 1968 in Jamaica. After he was expelled from Jamaica he returned to Tanzania and that's where *How Europe Underdeveloped Africa* was written. He stayed there until 1974 and then returned to Guyana, which is where he is still based.

Wherever Walter Rodney has lived, he has taken a deep interest in the affairs of the country. He has tried to analyze them; he has written; he has given in-person presentations about these aspects, and he has actually participated in the political process in the countries. This is evident in this short book, *Groundings ...* . It is also evident in *How Europe Underdeveloped Africa*. There are also a number of papers he has written on Tanganyika. Currently he is working on *A History of the*

Guyanese Working Class, and is actually participating in the struggle of that class.

It is therefore to be expected that the events in Jonestown would be subjected to the same incisive scrutiny that is evident is his writings. This is the topic of his presentation this afternoon, and I now turn to Dr. Walter Rodney [applause].

Talk by Dr. Walter Rondey

Good evening everyone: It is always good to be introduced by one's countryman and by one's friend. I recall that on one occasion the prime minister of Guyana was to have addressed a conference and he was introduced by someone who chose to quote — somewhat haphazardly — phrases from Shakespeare about individuals who are born great or achieve greatness or have greatness thrust upon them — you will recall the quotation. And he said that the prime minister of Guyana qualified in all three ways [laughing].

Walter Rodney from an illustration by Brian Rodway

Now, that in itself is strange. But what is stranger still is that the individual who is making the introduction was the Ombudsman in Guyana; that is to say, the public official, the unbiased public official, to whom you would take a dispute which you have with the prime minister. So I hope that fortunately you and I have no dispute which has to be resolved by [the Ombudsman of Guyana].

Topic
I would say that taking my cue from his [Ewart Thomas'] very last remarks, I would remind you that I am in fact resident in Guyana, that I am attempting to lay work that reflects within that society, and that what I have to say, therefore, is specifically from that perspective. Indeed, the topic is entitled, "Jonestown: A Caribbean or Guyanese Perspective."

I say this at the beginning so that we start together, so that we have no false expectation, one of the other. I will offer, for instance, no explanation of the ministry of motive behind the mass murder and suicide in Jonestown. I will not pretend to cover any possible involvement of the CIA. I will not delve into the amazing sex life of Mr. Jimmy Jones. I have no interest in recounting the final moments of Jonestown. Those are issues which have been touched by others, sometimes satisfactorily, sometimes not so satisfactorily, but in any event they fall outside of my own purview.

Instead, I want to speak about Guyanese society, and in speaking about Guyanese society, secondly it will be possible to generalize about the type of society, the dependent colonial society of which Guyana is but one example. And thirdly, I would like us to reflect upon the relationship between this society and the dependent society, the relationship between metropolitan societies and ones like Guyana, the Caribbean, Africa, and the so-called Third World, which are peripheral within the internationalist capitalist system because there are relations which are integral, which are essential, which are recurring between this part of the world and my part of the world. And it is incumbent upon us not merely to understand our society in and of themselves but to understand them within the wider framework.

Why in Guyana?
Having said that, the question which has been posed by Guyanese and in Guyana with respect to Jonestown is essentially, why should it have happened in Guyana? Others will ask, why did Jonestown occur? We would ask, why did it occur in Guyana? Was it a mere quirk? Was it an accident in the absolute sense of that word that it defeats any logical understanding that it should have occurred in Guyana? And we would argue that it was no accident, that it was not incidental. It is essential to an understanding of that tragedy that Guyana provided the framework in which it occurred. And that it [the Jonestown tragedy] tells us a great deal about Guyanese society and about dependent, peripheral, neo-colonial, post-colonial societies of the type.

Lure of Foreign Personage
First of all, what is very general to many, I would say least of all of the post-colonial society, a feature which they have not shed since colonial days is a certain type of welcome, a certain uncritical welcome to that which proceeds from the metropole. It is a welcoming spirit which in some senses is worthwhile, is credible, and personable, but it also opens these societies to being conned. It opens these societies to all manner of misdeeds. For example, quite removed from

Jonestown, the sort of thing that occurs when a European or American businessman steps off a plane whether in Kingston or Accra and he carries with him the aura of the metropolitan society and that aura allows him to sell all manner of junk at inflated rates in our society because there is that presumption of benefits spreading from the metropole.

There is that overtone that goes with cultural [word not clear], which allows that particular individual to function so effectively in our society to the detriment of our own people. There is some of that in Jonestown and in the welcoming carpet which was laid out for the Reverend Jim Jones when he approached our society and our government with respect to the settlement at Jonestown.

Alienation of Leadership and Citizenry
More important still, however, would be the character of our state, of the specific post-colonial state which developed in Guyana, with its own peculiarities, but which at the same time is part and parcel of a series of third-world states which show a great deal in common, demonstrate many features in common, a state which has distanced itself from the mass of the producers and the mass of the citizens in that state. Spoken of in class terms, it is a state which is not only alienated from the working people and the peasantry of our region, of our country, but which has also increasingly alienated itself even from the middle strata, even from the so-called petite bourgeoisie, who, in objective terms, may be said to constitute the class from which the government was recruited.

Even that class finds that the actual mechanisms of the state, both coercive and non-coercive, are not in the hands of the middle class, and of course, even less so in the hands of the working class. They become mechanisms which are monopolized by a very tiny segment of the population, usually itself dominated by petite bourgeoisie concerns, usually engaged either explicitly or otherwise in an alliance with international capital, but concerned internally with the disciplining and control of the mass of working people in the society. That is their principal function, whether they carry it out through the conventional state apparatuses of the police and the judiciary, or through the other extended tentacles of the state into the media and into the spheres of education. The fact is that they have created at this particular historical juncture, something [resembling] an incontrollable monster.

One doesn't have the time to go into the whole theorizing about the state. One understands that the state is not separate from the society. But at this historical juncture, the youth of these new societies those who control the state are in fact in a position to exercise inordinate power, to twist the society and to manipulate the surplus, to manipulate culture, ideas, people and so on in their own narrowly defined interests.

I would like to suggest that this is very important for understanding Jonestown, and that Jonestown in turn helps us the better to understand the distance between colonial or post-colonial state and the mass of its subjects, the alienation between citizen and state and particularly between the working class citizens and the state.

Private and Secretive
Jonestown was essentially based upon a relationship between the Peoples Temple, or the hierarchy of the Peoples Temple, and a number of individuals within the government of Guyana. It was not even an official relationship between the Peoples

Temple and the government in the open legal sense that our parliament and our national institutions had validated and legalized the relationship between the Peoples Temple and the Guyanese people. It was a very narrow, specific relationship between members of the government, prominent members of the government, the prime minister, the deputy prime minister, the minister of foreign affairs, heads of the judiciary and police, ambassadors, specific individuals, controlling positions of public power in the context of the warped nature of our state, in the context of the lack of controls over that state on the part of the Guyanese people; these individuals established what proved ultimately to be a very aberrant relationship with the group which was recruited from outside of our society.

What is interesting is of course that the mass of the people in Guyana were deliberately excluded from knowledge of Jonestown. Some two years ago, one political group, which at that time was in fact part of a coalition of which I myself was a part, a group known as the Working People's Vanguard Party, raised particular questions and asked about the repeated rumors that had been heard. This group even queried: what was Jonestown, what was the extent of its holdings, what was its status, and what was the relationship between the Guyana government and the U.S. citizens who were resident at Jonestown?

In other words, they asked the kinds of questions that in fact were publicly and internationally raised after the holocaust of November, 1978. But at that time we received no answers, because it is the normal procedure in Guyana that the government offers no answers or explanations to its citizens. It is a government that is so distant from the population that the normal functioning of information flows in the society—that does not occur. What you take to be commonplace, that citizens have access to what is called public information, information that is both generated publicly and which is known to be in the public interest—such information becomes practically state secrets in Guyana, as well as in a large number of third-world countries.

Absence of Accountability
That is why I feel that the import of my remarks will extend beyond the boundaries of Guyana. These are states in which it is no longer possible to have national income figures, national account figures; no longer possible to get data on the state of employment or unemployment in the society. One is given a series of fictitious figures regarding the inflation rate and so on. The question of audited public accounts, which was standard procedure in the colonial days, in that every year, every ministry, every institution of the government which handled public funds would leave an account to the people from whom these funds derived and on whose behalf these funds were supposed to be exercised—has practically disappeared in independent Guyana. Even in the colonial days such practice used to be treated as standard procedure.

We still have an official who is called the Director of Public Audit. But never has there been a post which is a greater sinecure than the Director of Public Audit in Guyana. He has not produced an audit for some 8 or 10 years. And I imagine that the only way his job will be in danger is if he in fact dares to try and produce an audit of public accounts.

Framework for Fiasco
So it is against that background one must understand that, curiously enough, such a large settlement of non-Guyanese

could flourish inside the national boundaries and the government did not find it possible before the crisis, during the crisis or subsequent to the crisis, to offer to the Guyanese people any explanation whatsoever as to the terms under which that group resided in our society.

Whatever we know of Jonestown we know it through investigations that came through channels outside of the government. Many of our people know paradoxically only that which they had learned from the foreign press and foreign media. One of those paradoxes was that after the news broke in Guyana, the government in Guyana had suppressed the news of the tragedy for some forty-eight hours. As it began to leak through the international media, people in Guyana began calling abroad to friends and relatives in London and New York and Toronto saying, "Would you please tell us what is this that is happening inside of Guyana; we don't know." Ultimately the government bended when it saw that the news was too big to hold and our people were given the details.

It seems to me that that particular parameter is especially important; the parameter that in third-world countries it has now become the norm, not the exception, that people have no access to important public information on which they should base judgment about events in their society.

So Jonestown was, in this particular respect at any rate, possible because it was entered into in a context in which the Guyanese people had no control, nor did they have even the prerequisite of that control, which is information. We are assuming that whatever judgments one arrived at, the prerequisite for that judgment is the available information on which one would exercise that judgment.

No Official Inquiry
And our people were deprived of that before, during and since the crisis. The news blackout and the government's attempts to ensure that the people did not discover the essentials of Jonestown, that process still continued. There was a major public demonstration [in the city] just after the incident. This was blacked out of the media. Few people outside our country, even some people in our country did not know there was a major public demonstration where people were demanding that the government should investigate Jonestown.

Ultimately after the U.S. government itself announced it would investigate, the Guyana government very belatedly said it would appoint a commission of investigation. It did in fact appoint one of its judges to be the investigator, one of the types who would normally say that the prime minister has greatness thrust upon him from all directions ... [laughing]. And this individual has not yet began to constitute the administrative mechanism for the investigation.

[The Judge appointed was the head of the judiciary, Chancellor of the Judiciary, A. V. Crane, who in a rare act of defiance announced about August 1979 that he wanted nothing to do with Jonestown. Observers are of the opinion that the appointment was never formalized. — E.K.]

The incident, as you know, occurred in November of last year, and at the present moment the Guyana government has not yet began even to set up the administrative infrastructure to carry out an investigation into the incident.

A Tragedy Waiting to Happen

This is the type of situation, which I am suggesting, made a Jonestown possible. That is the first stage of my analysis. This kind of situation in Guyana predisposed—it made a Jonestown possible, it did not necessarily make it inevitable. We shall now proceed in a little while to see why it became more and more likely as time went on.

Materialist Pursuits

It became more likely because the state in Guyana, like so many other parts of the Third World, is not only alienated from the population, but implicit in that alienation is that it had become a mechanism for accumulation on the part of segments of the national petite bourgeoisie. There are individuals within the society who see the state as the principal means by which they would acquire wealth personally.

The variety of ways by which individuals can acquire wealth traditionally, ownership of land, ownership of various forms of private property which yield value of a particular type—these still exist in our society. But throughout the Third World the state has been asked to do more than simply referee the struggle between the owners of the various means of production and the working class, or the struggle between different types of capitalists. The state has become that agency which is being constantly utilized and constantly fought over by a number of contending agencies precisely because they are aware that it can be used as an instrument of accumulation. And all the more is this true when the state extends its functions beyond the so-called conventional or traditional functions with which it has been associated and begins to undertake direct political enterprises—which is of course the case in Guyana, as in so many other parts of the Third World.

Corruption

As an integral part of the means of accumulation in the Third World, we must consider the advent of corruption. Corruption to my mind is not an aberration in the Third World; it is part of the normative political behavior now established in the Third World. This has to be understood because every third-world country to which you go, whether it be Nigeria, or Ghana, Tanzania, Guyana, Jamaica, Trinidad and Tobago, you will see in the national press some discussion of corruption and people proposing ways in which they can remove this blemish of corruption. The premise is that corruption is alien to the system and that it requires a few techniques and a few more honest persons here and there, and you will get rid of corruption.

For example, in Guyana when we had a lot of problems, the government decided that they would appoint an ombudsman to look into instances of corruption. And then the problem became: who would supervise the ombudsman [laughing]. Because the corruption being so endemic, it must really be seen as part of the means by which those who control the state in the Third World do not in fact bother to draw distinction between the quote/unquote legitimate and illegitimate means of accumulation. Any means that flow logically from the monopoly of political power are considered as acceptable within the political framework. And things such as cut-backs, fraud, and the illicit removal of public funds, these are integral at the present time to the distorted third-world states. And of course, they have a tremendous significance because in a number of economies, Guyana's being included, the size of the economy is so small that when a significant amount of funds is removed from the public treasury, it makes a great deal of difference to national economic development. At the present moment Guyana is in the grip of an International Monetary Fund oversight. We are asking the IMF for a standby credit of twenty million dollars. To meet the demands of the IMF, more hardships would have to be imposed on the working class. And yet, the amount for which we are asking the IMF is actually less than the amount known to have been siphoned off in foreign exchange frauds in Guyana over the last five years.

There has been a series of foreign exchange frauds which have removed from the public treasury more than twenty million dollars. And yet we have now to turn and ask an international agency to replace this and to endure onerous conditions that you know about and to which I will in fact allude in a short while. What I am driving at here is that, as it were, there were all indications of corruption that is part of the third-world system.

Gold, Diamonds, and U.S. Currency

One automatically asks, now what was Jonestown in the context of the material corruption for which the government of Guyana is well known? And one knows that it was located in an area which gave access to the gold and diamond fields. One notes that there was a significant amount of gold discovered in the settlement at the time. One notes that foreign currency, that is, U.S. dollars, were present in that area in huge quantities. And in our society we are therefore speaking about gold, diamond, and hard currency, three commodities. Foreign currency is classified as a commodity because in our society foreign currency is a most scarce and valuable commodity in our context.

It was very clear, even without our knowing the details of the transactions, that there was a relationship between members of the government as well as a specific individual in his public capacity and the leadership of Jonestown, which was based upon the movement of these commodities. Every effort was made to ensure that the movement of these commodities would not be monitored. They did not go through the normal customs regulations. In fact they broke the laws—all the laws—of Guyana which have to do with the control of currency, and of gold and diamonds. People need to have a license to trade in gold and diamonds, for which the Peoples Temple had not applied. And you have to have in Guyana a permit to have even ten American dollars in your possession. An attempt to change currency one way or another constitutes a serious offence for which dozens—indeed hundreds—of Guyanese have been brought before the courts on foreign currency charges.

So when one sees the settlement left free to speculate in these three commodities and the frequent visits by upper echelons of the government, it doesn't require a great deal of perspicacity to recognize what was the nature of the material connection.

There was an incident reported shortly after the actual deaths had occurred. It was reported that the deputy prime minister and the wife of the prime minister had brought gold and currency from Jonestown to Georgetown in a plane. The government of Guyana was very incensed at the report and issued an official disclaimer of this story. It said it was not true that they brought gold and currency in the plane; it was merely that they traveled on the same plane which brought the gold and currency [laughing]. The fact that there was no one else on the plane [loud laughing] was not very important in their calculation.

Laying the Foundation
This backdrop of material corruption is important for laying the basis for why Jonestown becomes more and more possible. In other words, it was introduced without the knowledge of the Guyanese people. It proceeds without any supervision from the Guyanese people. And it proceeds in a direction in which so long as specific members of the government will get their cut from the transactions taking place, in a sense, anything goes; or anything could have gone on in that settlement, without incurring the ire or the concern of the government of Guyana, because their concern was with one thing. And this is precisely how the scenario was elaborated.

If we examine data that is fully accessible, quite apart from other things that we suspect to be true and other rumors that are current in Guyana, we know that Jonestown entered into part of the deeper corruption of Guyanese political and social life. By the "deeper corruption" I mean things that go beyond merely a transfer of money or of something valuable. [We are talking of a level of] corruption that makes it impossible for the state to function even within the narrow framework of the constitution which we presently have. I'll take two examples having to do with the police and the judiciary.

Immunity from Police
First, the police. It does appear that the security services expressed a certain amount of alarm over what was taking place in Jonestown. First of all, the army, to the best of our knowledge, was told it should be hands-off, that Jonestown was not an area into which they would normally go to conduct exercises and so on. And that matters dealing with Jonestown must be cleared in an entirely different fashion. The police was more concerned: apparently they heard reports. And it seems from

a variety of statements, which have not been denied—even by the government itself, including by the Commissioner of Police [Lloyd Barker] himself—that at some stage he [Commissioner of Police] dared to express his concern and to move to have certain things done. And the word came back to him that that was not his prerogative; that was not his function; in a word, hands-off. The word came from above, not from below. People below are not in the habit of giving orders to the chief police officer of a country. So the Police Commissioner got this order from some source, which is still unidentified. But we know that we have now the focus considerably when we understand that chief police officers only take orders from a certain height. And we know that within our government that limits it to very few individuals. He was told, hands-off!

He had an interview with a number of Guyanese citizens after the Jonestown massacre, as it is called. And in this interview he was asked: why it was that guns were present in such large numbers in Jonestown? Why it was that dangerous drugs were present because they too fall under our legislation? Why it was that [U.S.] currency was there? Why they have machinery for which they have no license? Why it was that their boats came and went without going through Guyanese customs? What was the role of the police in all this? Etc. And he gave a very serious reply. He said that people get the police protection which they deserve.*[The Commissioner actually said everyone gets the police "surveillance" that he deserves. —E.K.]*

One has to place this [Police Commissioner's statement] in a broader context of the way in which the police harass the citizens of Guyana. And one infers from that that he was saying that whatever protection—that in effect, Jonestown did not need protection. It was being protected by the political elite, that the political elite had been ... that they should proceed in the way in which they were proceeding, and he did not feel as the chief police official that the people of Jonestown needed any protection. A very remarkable statement. And one bears in mind that under international law as well as under the conventions which guide people in any society it is normally accepted that when one moves into a new country, into a different country, one automatically receives the protection that that state has to offer. But our chief police official determined that the people of Jonestown did not need or deserve any protection. And this of course is because of that wider corruption in which it is possible for a phone call to be made to a high public official and for him to automatically—immediately—desist from carrying out his legitimate functions.

Subversion of the Judicial Process
With the judiciary, it was just as bad. It was clear that in the case of the Stoen child [John Victor Stoen], that now famous—or infamous—case, a notorious case that came over from the courts here [in the U.S.] to the courts of Guyana, that at least one judge in Guyana was prepared to order that the child be taken into the custody of the court. Because if there was a dispute, as there was, over the custody of the child, then the procedure, which we have inherited from English law (may or may not be the same here) is that the court shall in the interim exercise custody over the child. So one of those judges *[Aubrey Bishop, now deceased—E.K.]* sought to take the Stoen child from the Rev. Jim Jones and maintain the child in the custody of the court.

The record shows that he was frustrated in this enterprise by the Registrar of the court [Kenneth Barnwell], an important public official; that he was frustrated by political interference;

that he was actually receiving a number of threats. And ultimately he decided that under the circumstances he would wash his hands of the case. He made a public statement that he could not finally give judgment on the issue because a variety of methods were being used by parties on both sides, as he put it, to stop him from exercising his judicial judgment. And the case was given, returned, as is our practice, to the Chief Justice [Sir Harold Bollers], who is—who has the authority to reallocate that case to another judge. And under normal circumstances that authority would have been exercised to ensure that justice was being done. It would not have been possible to tolerate undue delay. It would have been reallocated to another judge but it so happens that the matter was placed in abeyance. Our Chief Justice determined in his wisdom that it was not necessary to reallocate that case. And so the Stoen child, like so many other children, was murdered at Jonestown.

[It since leaked out that the Chief Justice Harold Bollers had dinner with Jim Jones on the eve of the trial in the company of a visiting professor of criminology Dr. David Dodd, a party uninvolved in the case and probably invited as a diversion and an alibi.—E.K.]

Preventable Disaster

So really when one looks at the scenario from our perspective, we the Guyanese people recognize the way in which as the days went by Jonestown—without our knowledge, because most of this comes from hindsight, very few people has access to this information beforehand but as we saw it in hindsight—Jonestown, while it may not have been predictable was certainly preventable. We mustn't get involved in mysticism which says this thing is impossible to comprehend; how can human beings do this to themselves and each other. I don't know the answers to those questions. But those individuals were living in a specific society, and if that society was articulated in a particular way, their lives could not have been placed in danger as eventually occurred. It would have been prevented because so many abuses were known to have been occurring over the weeks and the months prior to the final debacle that something would have been done to put a stop to it.

In that sense, it would have been prevented. It would not have been prevented because someone foresaw that 915 people would have died, but they would have had to stop it because they would have said that this settlement is not in the national interest. They would have said that the rules governing the control, the authoritarian control by the leadership in this settlement over the various individuals, were not compatible with the rules governing the behavior of citizens, all citizens, in the society. They would, if they were serious about certain ideological pronouncements which they were making, they would of course have said that this was not a socialist settlement in the least. But all of these hypothetical preconditions did not exist. The government was not socialist. The government was not concerned about the lives of its own citizens and least of all about the common rank and file of the Peoples Temple. And so they allowed a certain situation to grow and grow until the final outburst with which all are familiar.

Jonestown, then, was preventable, and if it was to have been prevented, the principal agency in its prevention would have had to be the Guyanese government.

Government of U.S. not Blameless
The U.S. government bears a certain responsibility. And it is interesting to see that in the recent report which was here only a few days ago, there has been a cautious and guarded

recognition of that failure of responsibility on the part of the U.S. government. A citizen abroad is in a curious position. In a certain sense a citizen abroad is even more protected than a citizen at home because he or she falls under the protection of the host government as the first line of defence. If that host government fails to provide protection then they can have recourse to their own government, via its agencies, embassies, consulates, and so on. The people of Jonestown found that neither of these two lines of defence were of any use to them.

The government of Guyana was uninterested in their well-being, and the government of the United States reneged, for whatever reason, reneged on its function of entering to ensure that citizens abroad were being protected. So that, this tragedy is not the huge mystery that it has been made out to be. As a social phenomenon, Jonestown was most definitely preventable. While we may wish to ask the U.S. government some further questions, we are concerned with raising these questions to the Guyana government. It is still a political issue in our country.

Guyana Itself a Larger Tragedy
Now, it is of course part of the larger tragedy of Guyana. Jonestown merely came at a juncture when the national life was reeling from a series of blows. The economy is at a lower ebb than ever. The national balance is at a negative figure. There is inflation beyond all acceptable proportions. Unemployment spirals. Social violence increases. The moral fiber of the society begins to collapse in a most all-encompassing manner. One of the biggest issues in Guyana today among the population is how to get out. It is a society that is fast losing confidence even in its own ability to continue to persist, and a large proportion of people are seeking to escape from the society. Not

in Guyana alone; of course, a number of Caribbean societies are going through the same crisis to a greater or lesser extent. I remember that some wit I was told in Jamaica chalked up a slogan asking the last person to leave the island to please turn the lights off [laughing], because it seems as though that is the direction in which it was going. In Guyana the government has long since switched off the electricity so we don't have that problem [loud laughing].

But essentially, as part of a larger tragedy, which of course we as Guyanese … [tape abruptly ends].

Chapter 10

Jonestown Revisited

Jan Carew

Kalinyas, the Carib Kaseek, was my great-uncle and he had agreed to take me to the Jonestown site long after the tragic events there had shocked the world. We stood on a hilltop above the Kaituma River and while waiting for Trios, Kalinyas' grandson, to join us, we looked up at the sky and saw a convention of Harpy Eagles circling high above us. The cloudless sky was a hard, icy blue that absorbed and diffused some of the sun's fury.

"They're usually solitary birds, those great eagles, and we should know this in our bones, because they're our relatives," the old man explained matter-of-factly, shading his eyes with a gnarled hand that was networked with veins like shallow roots. "But since the event," he continued, and he invariably referred to the mass suicides at Jonestown as *the event*, "they gather every year to contemplate the thousand spirits that cannot find a resting place."

He meant *commemorate* but the old man had his own original way of what he called "mashing up the English language," and if I tried to correct him, he simply ignored me. I did not try this time. But I thought that perhaps, more than any people on earth, the Caribs understood the business of mass suicides. The curving chain of emerald islands that separates the Sea of the Caribs (the Caribbean) from the Atlantic, has many sites where, faced with the choice of slavery or death, the Caribs had chosen death. There is Morne Sauteur in Dominica, Carib's Leap in Grenada, Mount Pele in Martinique, Manzanilla in Trinidad—all of these sites bore silent witness to Carib mass suicides. The women suffocated their babies against their bosoms, and men, women and children sang their death songs before leaping over the cliffs. The Caribs died singing that new generations of fighters would arise from the blood-seeds of their sacrifice.

"The spirits of the thousand strangers who died on our sacred Carib land are still very much alive. They roam uneasily inside a circle of pain. That's why the great eagles gather once every year to *contemplate* the event. Those were homeless folk living in an age of homelessness. They came here hoping to island themselves in a house of peace. But now their tormented spirits are doing an endless walkabout. They couldn't find a resting place here on earth, and they thought Heaven would open its doors to them, because that's what their lying leader told them," Kalinyas said.

He had a dark brown face that was webbed with lines like a contour map of our land of many rivers. I never knew how old Kalinyas was, but he reminded me of one of those ancient trees that becomes stronger and more indestructible with age. He had wide shoulders, a barrel chest and legs like tree trunks. And from wearing sandals all of his life, his toes had spread out so comfortably that none of them touched the other.

The great Harpy Eagles soared lazily on tides of the wind, and as if the Sky God had shot an arrow from the sky, one of them plummeted towards the earth. At the last minute it leveled off, skimming a grassy knoll, then it rose skywards again with a bushmaster snake in its talons. When it was halfway between its companions and the ground, it released the shining serpent. Another eagle, which had already detached itself from the winged gathering, dived towards the bushmaster, struck it a blow to the head, retrieved it in its talons and the two flew away screaming their triumph like lost souls in a firmament of hell. An updraft lifted them higher until, banking sharply, they displayed the full splendor of their sun-silvered wings, and then they winged their way towards a distant nesting place to share the meal with a brood of young eaglets. Rooted to the spot, I felt a flicker of anxiety in my heart. The other eagles flew towards the sun until they became specks of dust against its incandescent orb of fire.

"It's a sign," Kalinyas declared. I waited for him to continue, but he didn't choose to enlighten me any further.

When I was a youth, and my parents had sent me to Aquero for summer holidays, Kalinyas had told me many times that our human souls were tied to Harpy Eagles by a spirit-knot, and I had believed him unquestioningly. But I had gone overseas for many years since that time, and now I had returned with an ingrained habit of disbelief. But the piercing scream of the eagles continued to echo and re-echo in my brain, and suddenly, it was as though fresh spring water had washed away the cobwebs of disbelief.

Trios joined us in the mid-afternoon. His moon-face was wreathed in welcoming smiles when he saw me. The last time

I'd seen him he was a babe-in-arms, and now he was a teenager attending college in Georgetown.

"So you, too, are being trained in the science of disbelief," I teased him.

"They say he's bright," Grandfather Kalinyas said deprecatingly, "but all they've taught him in those Georgetown schools can fit into the bottom of a thimble, and still leave plenty of room for my middle finger."

We were subjected to a ritual of purification when the sun fell like a stone behind the treetops. Our bodies were bathed in smoke from burning aromatic herbs, and we spent the night in a House of Silence. The hiss and crackle of burning logs grew fainter and fainter as the hours went by. The rustle of thoughts walking softly inside my head and the whisper of falling dew took me on journeys into the innermost sanctums of myself.

When morning came, my eyes looked outwards again and greeted the sunrise.

Kalinyas asked, "Are you ready, Manaharva?" *Manaharva* was my secret Carib name.

"I am ready, Kalinyas."

"Are you ready, Trios?"

"I am ready, Grandfather."

We went down to the river, washed ourselves, had breakfast and set out for Jonestown.

"I want you to see Jonestown with Carib eyes, and to feel it with a Carib heart," Kalinyas said.

"That's why I came, Kalinyas," I said.

"Grandfather alone saw everything and lived to tell the tale," Trios said soberly.

"Without your coming, Manaharva, I would have gone to walk amongst the stars, shackled by my secret forever," Kalinyas said.

"Uncle will write about it," Trios reassured the old man, "he's a writer. We study his books in school."

He had the old man's burning anthracite eyes and his massive and slightly stooped shoulders. Kalinyas had traveled from the distant Barima hills, the last sanctuary of the True Caribs, to rendezvous with us. I had taken that journey by river with him many years ago. But I still remembered the rhythms of the sun dance as our long canoe parted the dark, mirror-like waters of a network of rivers and creeks. Sometimes the sun appeared before us, but as the river meandered through green fastnesses, it would jump behind us. And it continued this hide-and-seek dance day after day.

We reached the Jonestown site after taking a shortcut. We paddled along a canal that bypassed some of Kaituma's meanderings.

"Through many seasons of moon, our Carib rainmakers brought heavy showers to redeem Jonestown from its shame and horror," Kalinyas explained as we followed a trail through swelling waves of undergrowth. It was clear that looters, vandals and souvenir hunters had inadvertently hastened a natural rhythm of decay and regeneration. Boardwalks between dormitories, cottages and community centers had rotted or had been thrust aside by the sprouting natural growths. There were only a few patches where the pink earth was still exposed and these looked like open sores. All of the buildings had been cannibalized for plumbing fixtures, roofing material, boards and furniture. But heaps of mildewed clothes, toys, shoes and hats had remained untouched. Abandoned shoes littering the area where the communal suicides had taken place were somehow the most poignant and vivid reminders of that apocalyptic tragedy.

As if to underline the point that Kalinyas had made earlier about what Carib rainmakers had done, a sudden downpour forced us to seek shelter under a tree with bright russet leaves. The rain ceased as suddenly as it had started. The wind gathered threatening rain clouds and herded them over an azure-rimmed horizon. The heat and humidity became more intense in the wake of the passing shower.

We continued until we came to the building that stood in what used to be the center of the community. Apparently, when the chanting worshipers gathered around this building, their shoes had fallen off when the final spasms of death had convulsed their bodies. Close to where the Reverend Jones and his wife had been found sprawled across steps leading to his private altar, a circle of shoes had been occupied by wild flowers and bromeliads that glittered like amethysts and rubies. In the center of the circle, a sapling had lifted a child's patent leather shoe a foot above the ground and it hung like a strange fruit that some rare and exotic plant had produced.

"You must write our truth," Kalinyas said fiercely.

I did not reply because I knew that he was ready to speak about *the event*. But another downpour drove us to seek shelter in a building with large jagged holes in the roof. For a while the atmosphere was suffocating, and then the rain stopped falling. Billions of drops of water dripping from wet leaves sounded like distant surf as the old man continued in a long stream.

"They wrote so many words about Jonestown! Those Yankee-people are strange. When they travel they want to carry the whole of their country on their backs. But look around you. Can you see how everything they left behind them is vanishing. This sacred land will be ours as long as a green skin covers the living world. When strangers tear away the green skin, the earth will be nothing more or less than a coffin for the dead. They came without knowing or wanting to know about the history of this Kaituma, heartland of the Caribs. This is a holy place for us, and no strangers have ever been able to stay here for long without making peace with our ancestors. The Spanish came in long time past days, and their colony vanished; then the Dutch came, and all that's left of them are the itabus that slaves dug to link up rivers and creeks; then the British came. For a while, it looked as if they'd leave us alone. But during a long and terrible drought, somebody found gold in a dry riverbed. He shouted the news of his find at the top of his lungs, and a storm of city folk descended on us. They picked up nuggets in the riverbed like shells on a beach. Unknown to them, though, the rains came over the country and deluged the far hills for weeks ... and one fine morning a wall of water fell on those miners and drowned them all. When the bodies floated up, some of the dead were still clutching nuggets in their fists. I know the spot where that disaster happened, but I'll die with the secret .... They wrote so many words about Jonestown," Kalinyas repeated, "but they wrote about themselves. For them, we were invisible, and yet, for the short season they were here I saw them without being seen. I was there the afternoon when death surprised them just as the sun was going down. They chanted and clapped hands for a while, and then there was a terrible silence. With candle flies in bottles to light my way, I walked amongst their dead. They'd died in circles like worshipers around invisible altars. The children were buried under the flesh of their mothers. All alone I sang the Carib death-songs, and afterwards, I called upon their spirits either to reconcile themselves with the spirits of our ancestral dead or go back to the land of their ancestors. I told them, 'No one among you bothered to ask the living Caribs and the spirits of their ancestors for permission to share their sacred land' and I shouted under the stars, 'Don't you know that this place we call Kaituma means the Land of the Everlasting Dreamers?'"

Trios said somewhat tritely, "The prime minister couldn't give our land to Jim Jones, because he didn't own it in the first place."

"They wrote about their folk living and dying here," Kalinyas continued, "We, the Keepers of the Land, the Everlasting Dreamers, were invisible to them. We are the Keepers of the dreams of the living and the dead, and yet they never said a word to us. What could they ever know about the smell of our sacred earth or the dreams of our people! You must write our truth, Manaharva!"

I   Members & Survivors

II   Residents & Visitors

III   Analysts & Critics

IV   Editor & Compiler   ✓

V   Appendix & Miscellany

Chapter 11

A State within a State

First published in *Dayclean* (Special Edition) 11-21-1978

Eusi Kwayana

On Saturday, November 18, 1978, two planes, one from the Guyana Airways Corporation (GAC) and another that was privately chartered, landed at Kaituma to pick up Congressman Ryan of the U.S., members of his staff, U.S. embassy officials, concerned relatives of members of the Peoples Temple and foreign newsmen and photographers. Congressman Ryan and the rest of his party had gone into Jonestown to investigate repeated complaints in the U.S. that people who wanted to leave the Peoples Temple were being held against their will.

Genocide at Peoples Temple
Dayclean is informed that just before the planes landed a member of the sect held a knife to the congressman's throat while he was still in the compound. When the planes arrived the pilots were told that there might be trouble. It was while the pilots were rounding up members of the party that a tractor-trailer was seen approaching from the bush. Four armed men from the trailer opened fire from eleven to twelve feet away. Five persons were killed, including Congressman Ryan, three news people and a member of the Peoples Temple.

Several others were wounded, some seriously. The GAC plane was shot up and could not take off.

The weapons used were described as modern and included high-powered automatic rifles and shotguns. The people shooting were said to be professional and fired like marksmen.

Three Guyana Defence Force (GDF) men who were on the airstrip during the shooting were appealed to for help. They refused and took cover in the bush. The two pilots and other survivors of the murder attack fled in the small plane while others in the party, including an eight-year-old boy, were left behind. Some fled into the surrounding bush.

Masthead of *DayClean*, newsletter of the Working Peoples Alliance (WPA) — Artist: Brian Rodway

Reports of these events reached the highest levels of government on the very Saturday night. The next day, reports of mass suicide were received from a man who had escaped from the Peoples Temple at Jonestown. It took from Saturday night to Sunday night for GDF forces to enter Jonestown. They found no survivors. Hundreds of people, all members of the Peoples

Temple, were dead. Many of the dead had gunshot wounds. Others had been injected with poison. Later, members of the investigation team who had escaped into the bush during the "mass suicide" revealed that they had heard Rev. Jim Jones telling his followers, "Let's not fight among ourselves." This was followed by the sound of people running and screaming. Armed guards ringed the settlement during the "suicide." The "mass suicide" was in fact mass murder.

Meanwhile, in Georgetown, the public relations officer for the Rev. Jim Jones died along with her three children later on Saturday. Reports say that the woman's injuries could not be self-inflicted, that is, she could not have committed suicide.

No Information

In a press conference where the Minister of Information [Shirley Field-Ridley] answered the majority of questions with "I don't know," "I have never heard that," "I don't have the details," or "I don't have that information," the government continued the cover up. This began several months ago from the moment the Peoples Temple began to be exposed. The minister's statements included the following:

1. That members of the Peoples Temple were in Guyana as farmers, as part of the government's land settlement policy. Through that policy other groups and individuals from the U.K., the U.S. and the Caribbean had settled in Guyana.

2. That the farmers at Jonestown were industrious, had a good reputation, and obeyed the laws of Guyana.

3. That the government had received complaints against the Peoples Temple, but in the many letters received,

many of them were favorable to the Temple. The government therefore saw no reason to investigate the unfavorable complaints.

4. That government personnel had free access to and frequent contact with Jonestown in the normal course of their duties and saw no irregularities.

5. The GDF at the airport could not help because they were mechanics and non-combatants. Furthermore, they were probably confused as to what was happening.

6. That the GDF forces dispatched to Kaituma on Saturday night did not reach until Sunday night because the 5- to 6-mile road between Kaituma and Jonestown was in bad condition and the weather was bad.

7. That many details on the incidents were not yet known because telephone communications between Kaituma and Jonestown were bad because the weather was bad.

8. That the government was having a logistical problem getting bodies out of Jonestown and getting military and medical personnel into Jonestown.

9. That the Minister of Information:

    - Was not aware that in the past foreign newsmen were being denied entry to do stories on the Peoples Temple.

    - Never heard that ships left Jonestown without passing customs.

- Had not been told that some of the concerned relatives going to Jonestown had asked for police protection.

There were other foolish statements, more notably that we should not prejudge the character of the Peoples Temple (not even that there was something sinister going on). Then, there was a promise to compile what they called "a register of the dead." All in all, the minister bungled the cover up.

No Excuse

Reports in the local press seem to be stressing Jones's recent behavior. "He went mad." This seems to be the view of his lawyer, Charles Garry, a well-known U.S. radical, who was always strong in the praise of Jones. It would appear that he is having difficulty explaining why he earlier saw no negative tendencies. If that is going to be the government's line as well it won't work. No interpretation can excuse the government. What the Guyanese people must understand is that it is not a question of this or that. It is quite possible for a place to be a farm and a training ground.

The Regime Stands Accused

The regime stands accused of criminal negligence. Whether or not it is true that no investigation was ever held by the regime against Jones, the attitude of the regime was consistently negligent about the implications of these allegations. In a recent interview with foreign news correspondents, the Minister of Education dismissed complaints about Jonestown on the ground that those things could not happen in Guyana. He added, as if in evidence, that he had recently visited Jonestown for two hours. Did he investigate? Did anybody investigate?

Are we to understand that because Jones came highly recommended (some say by Angela Davis, others by Rosalynn Carter, the U.S. President's wife) that the Guyanese government is freed of the responsibility to investigate the people it brought to settle on Guyanese land?

The regime stands accused of criminal greed. There is evidence that the Peoples Temple brought at least $36,000 into the country each month from the Social Security checks of pensioners who were members of the Temple. There are reports of payoffs to the ruling party and to certain individuals. Now, we find that they are discovering rice bags filled with money of local currency, gold and diamonds.

The regime stands accused of criminal conspiracy. The ruling party could not have been ignorant of the piling up of modern weapons at Jonestown. It must have heard about the armed force which carried out regular drills. We believe that the regime actively supported this accumulation of arms because it could use the arms if needed or if its regular forces proved unreliable.

The regime stands accused of criminal arrogance. It believed wrongly that it could control the kind of man Jim Jones was often accused of being—a madman and a criminal masquerading as a socialist and manipulating his following to blind obedience.

Unanswered Questions
The Guyanese people are asking the following questions:

1. How was original contact with Jim Jones made?

2. Was there an investigation into the Peoples Temple before thousands of acres of Guyanese land were leased to them?

3. Why was a town named after Jim Jones (Jonestown)?

4. What was the status of Jones and other foreign residents vis-a-vis Guyanese Immigration laws?

5. What was the status of children born in Jonestown?

6. Were these births recorded in the official Guyanese Registry of Births?

7. Were these children not Guyanese?

8. If so, why were we told that there were no Guyanese involved?

9. Was any record kept anywhere of those who entered the country to settle in Jonestown?

10. Following allegations of people held captive at Jonestown and of acts of violence at Jonestown, did the government of Guyana have the police investigate "in the normal course of their duties"?

11. Why was the Peoples Temple allowed to operate a ham radio in violation of international conventions?

12. Was the government informed that this radio sent coded messages between Georgetown, Port Kaituma and the United States?

13. Did the government know that Jonestown was also violating Guyana's laws relating to currency, customs, immigration, and weapons?

14. Did the government intervene in the child custody case against the Temple?

15. If so, is it true that it intervened after threats of mass suicide at Jonestown?

16. Did the government restrict the army and the police from carrying out normal investigation and security functions not only before, but during the events this weekend?

17. Why did our news stations announce developments this weekend only after the BBC did so?

18. Is it being assumed that none of the killers in the mass murder this weekend are among the survivors or "defectors"?

19. Is there no danger to eyewitnesses and investigators still in Guyana?

20. Is it true that Jones made an international call from Kaituma at 3:00 a.m. on Sunday and that this call was monitored by the police?

21. Are the police checking into the possibility that some did not take part in the "mass suicide"?

22. Have all the times of death been identified?

23. What is the relation of the government to similar groups like Rabbi Washington's House of Israel?

Let us hope that with the passage of time there will be answers to these questions.

Postscript:
I reproduced the above exactly as I wrote it shortly after the disaster. Some of the questions I asked then have been answered over time and some still remain unanswered. In a crisis of this magnitude early reporting is bound to be deficient as seen over time. However, I wanted to maintain the fidelity of the report at the critical time of its appearance, thus the report as it was published the first time.

Chapter 12

Placing Guyana on History's Map

Eusi Kwayana

The Jonestown catastrophe is said to have placed Guyana on the map of history as no other event, before or since. Lest one should think that Jonestown is the only event that drew the world's attention to this country, I shall cite a few other examples from our history. I shall also explain how this book is different from other books on the subject as well as what purpose it is expected to serve.

Geography 101
But first, a quick geography lesson. Guyana, selected by Rev. Jim Jones of the Peoples Temple as a "Promised Land" for his voluntary exiles from the USA, lies on the northern edge of the South American continent. It nests between Venezuela on its west and Suriname on its east, and is troubled by territorial claims from each of these neighbors. Similar claims from Brazil were settled between Britain and Brazil, which gained approximately 6,000 square miles of territory from the British colony.

The geographer Leslie Cummings (Cummings: 1965) follows the weather patterns given by previous Guyanese geographers like De Weever and Moore[1]: two wet and two dry seasons. Cummings (Cummings: 1965) refines them as a long rainy season (mid-April to mid-August), followed by a long dry season (mid-August to mid-November), and succeeded by a short rainy season (mid-November to mid-February), and then a short dry one (mid-February to mid-April).

Northwest District and El Dorado
Cummings (Cummings: 1965) recorded the coffee-growing potential and the gold-mining possibilities in parts of the Northwest District. In listing the coastal roads then existing, he mentioned Morawhanna-Wanaima, 13 miles in length, but did not include the railroad and third-rate road, said locally to be about 30 miles long, extending from Matthews Ridge to Port Kaituma. (The small entertainment center known as "Bottom Floor" was one of the busiest places on the road.) This now abandoned railroad was laid by the African Manganese Company in later colonial times to transport supplies of the ore to the company's shipping dock. Manganese ore was discovered in the Matthews Ridge area, Northwest District, around 1903 and the ore was mined from 1960 to 1969.

Cummings also recorded that the railway extended from Matthews Ridge to the shipping canal at Port Kaituma. He spoke of an earlier time when oceangoing boats had to make "the long journey through the Mora Passage and up the Kaituma River."

---

1   *The reference is to Aloysius De Weever, who wrote in 1927 "A Textbook of the Geography of British Guiana, the West Indies and South America."*

Dimensions from a Guyanese Perspective

In order for the Peoples Temple's oceangoing craft to ply the route from the USA to Port Kaituma, Jim Jones must have done painstaking research and investigation through the forerunners of these trade routes, unknown to the present urban generations. Such forerunners come into the story told by Desmond Andrews (see Chapter 3, "As Seen by Bystanders,") in a brief interview with me.

A careful reading of some of the non-sensational interviews given by Guyanese in this book will help readers to connect the death toll at Jonestown with the weather pattern, or it may not. Still, geography may sharpen the readers' grasp of all the prevailing circumstances.

Guyana was at first, at least in written history, a territory under the control and management of its indigenous peoples of various language groups. In Dr. Sylvia Wynter's[2] beautifully profound phrase, like all people everywhere, each group had its "ways of being human."

Several events over many years have "placed Guyana on the map." The English courtier-pirate[3] first in 1595 passed along its coast on the Atlantic and picked up a report that a golden city, El Dorado, lay in its interior. He published a best seller, *The Discoverie of Guiana*. This book, translated into several European languages, had the effect of starting a post-Columbus race for gold to the whole Guyana area.

Shifting Loyalty

Guiana (its name before 1966) was by the 1830s a string of three Dutch colonies, stolen from their first nation indigenous

---

2   *Jamaican novelist, dramatist, critic, essayist and academic.*
3   *The reference is to Sir Walter Raleigh.*

owners by various European invaders. Essequibo, the oldest, joined with Demerara in 1789. Berbice was founded by the Van Pere family in 1627 as a separate colony. Corporations today make up their faces against state ownership. In the seventeenth century chartered corporations owned and operated plantations in the tropics and especially in the Caribbean and the Americas. In Guyana, the Caribbean and North America, the Dutch West India Company (DWIC) was both the monopoly producer and the government at one and the same time. The DWIC had a charter from the Dutch States General, which, in the place of God, gave the company full power to go into foreign countries and seize territory, dominate populations, capture, enslave, and trade in human cargo, dispense justice and make as much money as possible. All self-respecting European Christian powers engaged in the activity. Guyana became known again and again, during European wars of rivalry. In 1812 when the United Kingdom and the young USA were at war, the USA patrolled Guiana's waters and blocked her ports. When the wars came to an end, some Caribbean countries, all colonized, changed overlords. Even the slave owning class was totally ignored. They and their property woke up the morning after the peace treaty and found that they owed allegiance to a new sovereign. This arrangement assured that some balance of power elsewhere was adjusted to suit the victors. This is another way in which Guyana was "put on the map."

1763 Uprising
In 1763 the enslaved Africans of Berbice, starting on the privately owned plantations, launched a new kind of uprising. I have called it a revolution because the African leaders had declared in a letter to the Dutch Governor, Wolfert Simon Van Hoogenheim, "but we shall not be slaves again." The

revolutionaries held the territory for eleven months, proposed a division of Berbice, one of the parts, being under a black governor. Finally, Dutch warships bringing new arms and soldiers came into the scene and drowned the uprising in blood. Clearly this event brought Guyana to the notice of the literate Europeans and more gradually to the notice of the rest of the world, placing the colony "on the map" in a new way.

1823 Uprising
Uprisings led by the enslaved captives were many. In 1823 there was a classic uprising on the East Coast of Demerara. Active in its leadership were many of the leaders of Bethel Chapel, Rev. John Smith's Church at Le Resouvenir. Smith was the second minister posted to Demerara by the London Missionary Society. Quamina and Jack Gladstone, deacons of the church, were among the best-known leaders of the grass roots uprising. Organized on every plantation, it coincided with agitation in England for ending the genocidal system. The colonial state in Guyana implicated Rev. John Smith in the activity which they deemed treasonous and charged Smith with concealment of the plot. Smith was imprisoned for treason. Governor Murray of Demerara ordered a trial for the Rev. John Smith, who, by teaching his congregation to read, had first offended the governor and earned a threat of banishment. Smith was found guilty. He remained in jail suffering from tuberculosis and died while awaiting the final decision on his sentence from London. He became for the Church, the Martyr Smith, although the Reverend Canon W. G. Burgan, M.A., declared in a sermon at St Augustine's Anglican Church in the 1950s that Smith had become a martyr "by a mere fluke." These events again "put Guyana on the map," especially in church and parliamentary circles in London.

(For the most recent and most ample study of 1823 event, refer to *Crowns of Glory, Tears of Blood* by the Brazilian scholar Emilia Viotti da Costa.)

1834 Act of Emancipation
Guyana again found "a place on the map" in 1834 at the time of the British Act of Emancipation. As historians agree, the Slavery Abolition Act the year before (1833) required the former enslaved Africans to become free citizens, that is, no longer chattel, but with the "right" to forced labor for their former owner for a period of six years. Ex-slave Damon led a peaceful protest on the Essequibo coast against this deceptive freedom. Whole plantations in Essequibo were disappointed and suffered much surveillance. Damon and a selected band of dissenters occupied the churchyard at La Belle Alliance and held a night's vigil, refusing to chant or to speak. In retrospect, this was an early example of passive resistance, so passive that the uneasy militia found no pretext for action. However, Damon and a few others were arrested as ringleaders, and tried as a formality. Damon was sentenced to death and hanged. He was the first named martyr of the post emancipation period. Others were banished from the colony. The event is covered by Hugh Payne in *The Ten Days that Changed the World*. This was another case in which Guyana "was placed on the map."

1953 Intervention
In the twentieth century, Guyana was to be "put on the map" again in 1953. After three decades of labor struggles and political agitation for the right to vote, the multi-ethnic population came together in 1950 to form a political party, the People's Progressive Party, the party pioneered by Cheddi Jagan. Despite the well-publicized Marxist convictions of some of its best-known leaders, the party was an anti-plantation coalition

aiming at self-determination. In 1953 it won 18 of the 24 seats in the new House of Assembly in the first election held under universal adult suffrage. This election victory at once brought the colony "within the sphere of influence of the United States of America." After 133 days following the elections victory, there was another graduation to the world map when the British gunboats landed troops and supported the governor in the dismissal of the elected ministers as ordered by the Colonial Office. Guyana found itself again "on the map of the world."

The Greatest Peacetime Tragedy
Guyana's political process was for the most part peaceful. Yet, it was bedeviled by racial rivalry, and leaders treated this malaise as secondary. Long before the coming of Jim Jones, it had experienced four years of inter-ethnic violence which had got worse year after year up to 1964. This conflict had some cold war involvement and was received abroad differently by different audiences. These incidents arose from colonial manipulation over a century and more and the short-sightedness of political leaderships. The tragedy of November 18, 1978, was specific in form. Walter Rodney in 1979 best explains why the tragedy became possible in Guyana. (See his analysis in Chapter 9, "Jonestown: A Caribbean / Guyanese Perspective.")

The events of November, 1978, more than any other brought Guyana to the notice of the world, to political and non-political, religious and non-religious people alike, to those who listened to the news and to those who did not. It was the violent death of some 900 members of the Peoples Temple at Jonestown, the Temple's "Promised Land" in Guyana, which the Rev. Jim Jones had called the "mission field."

In 1973 Rev. Jim Jones obtained a lease for the Peoples Temple of some 3,000 to 4,000 acres of land in the Northwest District of the country. Within two years succeeding batches of Templeites were settling on the project, aiming at creating a self-sufficient type of commune. As in the USA, the Peoples Temple was officially a church, but in practice, a social justice movement. It impressed non-whites with its policy of embrace of those who were rejected in the official society. The spirit and the postures of the membership, mainly black and white, convinced a significant number of African Americans that within it they could realize their dream of equality.

The story of how the Peoples Temple's Promised Land in Guyana destroyed itself on November 18, 1978, has had as much reporting as the outbreak of any war. Tensions were perceived between the leadership and the majority of its followers. Yet, in spite of everything they thought, they took no action against Rev. Jim Jones. The violent death of over 900 members of the commune, some hours after the murder of Congressman Ryan and a number of defectors, stunned the world. *The Jonestown Massacre, The Suicide Cult, Raven, Snake Dance, Six Years with God*—books rolled off the presses. The murder/suicide of all of these people in the age of satellite reporting put Guyana on the map in a way it would not have chosen.

The Aim of this Book

This book attempts to do simple tasks. It tries to show why the government of Guyana and the Peoples Temple chose each other. It offers Guyanese responses to the events which reached a bursting point on November 18, 1978. It explains the place of Peoples Temple in the political economy of Guyana at a season of state deformation. It gives snatches of the experience as recalled by Guyanese and not caught in most of the externally written accounts. It examines some of the testimony of survivors and surviving records and makes comments that appear necessary, raising some new questions.

It compares the sophisticated operations of the white-led Peoples Temple with two other efforts by U.S. citizens in Guyana. One was a small agricultural settlement of African Americans to engage in agriculture without the resources of the Peoples Temple. The other was The House of Israel led by an African American. It shows how the House of Israel was religious and political, and played a very negative enforcer and thug role in Guyanese politics without however recording any mass killings of its own members. Finally, this book hopes to make a new assessment of Jim Jones, as revealed from the point of view of citizens of the host country.

This book deals with the very sensitive and important modern problem of human relations. People have always been coming and going sometimes without planning to. The book is not about hostility to foreign-born people. Dr. Barbara Josiah (Josiah: 2011) names African Americans who came to the colony British Guiana as business people and as engaged workers in the 19th and 20th centuries and were most welcome by their hosts. As the women's movements have taught us, it is always the "power relations" that matter in the majority of cases of relations between different peoples. This was one of the issues in Jonestown internally, and between it and the wider society.

Chapter 13

On Jeannie Mills' Book *Six Years with God*

Eusi Kwayana

There is a closeness between the time when Prime Minister Burnham in 1973 took a decision to shut down and disband about thirteen cooperatives of African Guyanese and the time when presumably the arrangements with Jim Jones began to come on stream. In San Francisco in 1973, Jim Jones was talking about the "Promised Land," which he sometimes named as Guyana.

Six Years with God by Jeannie Mills (Mills: 1979) is not a popular book, but it has its value regardless of later conduct alleged against the author. The book reports that Jim Jones had explained that because he was setting up the "new mission field" in Guyana he could not offer the customary financial supports to her or certain members of the Temple. In another place she reports Jim Jones as saying that he had secured 3,000 to 4,000 acres of land in Guyana and that he was rather uneasy, as Dr. Reid, the Deputy Prime Minister, had suffered a stroke, even though he was conscious. According to her, Jones had described Dr. Reid as closest to the Temple's affairs. Dr. Reid had in fact suffered a stroke, but had returned to office in due course. In this and other ways Jim Jones introduced the affairs of the government of Guyana into his conversations at the Peoples Temple in San Francisco, California, USA. From his vantage point and his relations with his favorite ministers of the government, he could pick up gossip about developments in the leadership of the PNC, the ruling party, which in 1974 declared its "paramountcy" over the state. Much of this information was not known to the Guyanese people, but became matters for speculation between Jones and his followers. Although Ms. Mills and her crew are less than favorites of Temple people, all the things she revealed in the passage above as said by Jim Jones about Guyana are factual.

Jones revealed (December 5, 1975) that he wanted to have his lease in writing and was prepared to travel to Guyana at short notice to achieve this.

Khaleel Mohammed, a Guyanese scholar in Comparative Religion and Professor in Religion at San Diego State University, said that Burnham very likely wanted the example of Jonestown with its majority of African-American settlers as a way of appealing to the African Guyanese supporters of the PNC.

This writer, Mills, got the impression that the right to go to the Promised Land was available on questionable criteria. It was open, the writer claimed, to those "with legal difficulties or those who are beginning to act hostile against the church ... ."

My own interviews with survivors did not confirm Mills's claim. Yet it was clear that Jones determined who went. There will be many reasons for an approving authority in such a political enterprise where undertakings to a foreign government may be a factor. But whether this prevented persons with too much independence from going to Guyana is important, especially in the light of the perils of obedience at the heart of the tragedy.

On page 46 of the book is a claim that a member mentions to James that Jones had been shipping weapons to Guyana in the bottom of crates marked "agricultural supplies." Members were also arriving in Guyana with money tied around their waists and both cases of bad faith were devices to avoid the scrutiny of the Guyana customs. Much of this can be confirmed from what was found at Jonestown after it imploded. Mills did not know that Peoples Temple members arriving in Guyana at Timehri Airport had advanced clearance and were not subject to the usual procedures. Goods like weapons, therefore, were not perhaps taken in with passengers but concealed in incoming legitimate crates as suggested in the book. The paranoid prime minister of Guyana was not about to permit the entry of arms into Guyana except through an agreement approved by him and in his control. It is likely that these goods had been shipped in the Temple's own high seas craft.

Jones's bad faith in the 1970s as recorded in *Six Years with God* shows Jim Jones as a professing revolutionary leading the practice of "apostolic socialism." Guyana had since 1966 the severest gun laws in the Caribbean, under which, once the National Security Act had been activated, a person found with a mere band to keep bullets steady could be subject on conviction to life imprisonment. No government in the so-called Third World would have consented to guests arriving with hidden weapons. Further, such an act would be seen as a breach of faith and as disregard for the host country. It was either that Burnham gave clearance for the Temple members to bring weapons or he did not. If he did there would be no reason to hide the weapons in order to bring them to Guyana. Burnham, somewhat like Jones and other maximum leaders, would want to know everything. He once famously boasted in the context of a public statement to Amerindian Toshaos[1]. He said that although he was prime minister of the country he knew what took place in the remotest parts of the country, and referring to missionaries, gave as an example, "how they come with bibles and leave with gold."

Peoples Temple was a white-led religious/political organization whose claims to religion and to revolution need to be briefly evaluated. In the world of the seventies, rich with uprisings of the downtrodden, there was among valid groups much revolutionary honor, with and without arms. Governments all over Africa, even when considered not revolutionary, not democratic or helpful to their own citizens, would often give safe conduct, shelter or sanctuary to revolutionaries fighting for their independence, or wishing safe transit through their territories. On no account would transits in that state or their organizations violate the trust of the facilitating government.

Coming into being not more than three years before the arrival the Peoples Temple was the House of Israel, led by an African American, who came to Guyana after, as he claimed, he had previously gone to Algeria. Unlike Jim Jones, who, according to Concerned Relatives, had escaped prosecution for breaches of human rights in California, Washington had skipped bail after conviction for fraud. Washington also lacked the carefully cultivated relations that Jim Jones had with the elected officials that mattered.

---

1 *Head or chief of the Amerindian community in Guyana 1952 – 1992.*

As surprising as it may seem, there were no charges pending against Jim Jones when he left California, nor any findings of criminal behavior by him, after the deaths in Jonestown.

Temple members as well as former officials testify that Jones's well-wishers were well distributed in the government systems in northern California. The African American of the House of Israel was not so well organized among the elected officials of Cleveland and had been sentenced there for fraud, after leading a successful boycott of a McDonald franchise which did not employ African Americans.

At a certain stage of the anti-dictatorial struggle, one year after the implosion of Jonestown, the army, that is the Guyana Defence Force (GDF), on the instructions of its then commander-in-chief Mr. Burnham, handed over self-loading rifles (SLRs), to the House of Israel. *Dayclean*, the organ of the Working People's Alliance, obtained and published documentary evidence of the delivery.

Although many denied the validity of the documents displayed at a press conference by the WPA to sustain the charge of the arming of the House of Israel, the Rabbi admitted the delivery to Andrew Morrison, SJ. The quotation that follows is from his book: *Justice: The Struggle for Democracy in Guyana, 1952 - 1992*. "Asked if the House of Israel had received a quantity of arms and ammunition from the army, as the WPA had reported, he [Rabbi Washington] readily agreed" (Morrison, 1998, p. 174).

At length it was shown that the number of arms held by Jonestown was recorded at 42 pieces. [The number of pieces actually recovered was 32.] Both the GDF and the Guyana

Police Force seemed to agree on that number. Mr. Burnham would not have allowed an undisclosed number of weapons to be imported and stored outside of his control. He might have adopted various other devices in order to keep an armed squad at Jonestown. He could easily have established a unit of the Guyana People's Militia, essentially a PNC force, at Port Kaituma or Matthews Ridge and could have arranged participation for Jonestown. He could have given official arms to the Jonestown leaders, officially, but illegally. Burnham did rely on several armed forces:

- Guyana Police Force
- Guyana Defence Force
- Guyana National Service
- National Guard Service
- People's Militia
- Young Socialist Movement
- Women's Revolutionary Socialist Movement (WRSM)

I have seen disclaimers from the Women's Revolutionary Socialist Movement (WRSM). My evidence regarding the WRSM is that they marched with arms in public parades on a few occasions and their photos appeared in the government-owned newspaper. Perhaps they were not in fact an armed unit. If they were not in fact an armed unit, they were officially slandered.

My first response and my opinion for some years was that Burnham was aware of the presence of arms in Jonestown and consented to it on the grounds that they could be used in his favor. Having had the chance to study Jonestown and Jim Jones more closely from the Jonestown Institute (Jonestown, web site) and other sources and from interviews, I have changed my views on that subject.

There is no suggestion of the Temple using its arms against Guyanese. There is testimony that on November 18, when the massacre of the intruders and dissidents took place at Kaituma, the Temple's guards purposely did not aim at a single Guyanese although some of them, journalists, were in firing range. Guyanese journalists could have done as much damage to Jone's reputation as U.S. journalists, except that Guyanese state journalists were all under the control of the Minister of Information and enjoyed little freedom to report unfavorable incidents even though they made news, without the permission of the censors. Mr. Burnham had made a famous statement when he was challenged in Barbados in 1973 on repressing freedom of information. He had said, "In Guyana we don't tell people what to print; we tell them what *not* to print."

For a professing revolutionary and also as the voice of "apostolic socialism," Jim Jones chose an odd season to be embedded in Guyana. He could not be unaware of the fact that the ruling party of Guyana had committed a record takeover of the parliament by rigging the general elections to the extent of a two-thirds majority. To dramatize this charge against the PNC, it should be clear that the PNC defeated the PPP in its traditional stronghold of sugar workers and rice farmers, both mainly of Indian origin. If this were so, then that would have been the end of racial voting in Guyana. The general elections of 1980 were to further diminish the PPP in parliament, reducing it to 14 seats of the total of 65. These fake majorities were to evaporate when because of the struggles of the anti-dictatorial forces—not necessarily democratic forces —the counting of the votes at the place of poll was imposed, putting an end to the kidnapping and transporting of ballot boxes to forbidden places of custody.

Into this domestic political squalor Jim Jones found it convenient to implant his powerful movement for reform. It will be noted that Jones had landed in a dual ethos to which he was already accustomed. Part of the reason for his timing the departure from the USA was doubtless the gradual exposure of the underbelly of the otherwise highly reputable and politically "progressive" Peoples Temple. Jones, its prophet, had left San Francisco in a cloud of suspicion. It is interesting that survivors are still devoted to the ideals of Peoples Temple. And the title of this book (my book) could be "Jim Jones versus Peoples Temple."

Mills records that several church members had been placed on criminal charges for beatings and other forms of abuse. The beatings were public and reinforced with preaching. A leader whose great heart melted at a child's abuse of an insect would order as many as a hundred lashes for a human being. Members who had grown dissident would shudder as Jones deftly asserted the point that at Peoples Temple there were no beatings.

Postscript:
Unlike the CIA which had long been attacked by the forces of the free movements and investigative and human rights journalism as notorious, the KGB had enjoyed a sheltered existence, to the extent that the public was unaware of its presence in the Soviet Embassy in Georgetown, Guyana.

When the Peoples Temple moved to Guyana and finally imploded on November 18, 1978, the tragic end was unreported in the government-controlled Guyana press and radio for as long as possible. The speech by Dr. Walter Rodney, delivered with humor and disgust but no bitterness, forms a chapter in this book and shows his grief at the anti-information culture, then a mode of policy in too many developing countries, Guyana included. In this vein, an African head of UNESCO, Mr. Mbau of Gambia, had warned newly independent countries, "We make no distinction between external and internal repression."

Up to November 18, 1978, the state-controlled *Chronicle* had carefully shielded the Peoples Temple and Jonestown from unfavorable reporting. The Temple, like another PNC-aligned organization, House of Israel, led this time by an African American, Rabbi Washington, enjoyed frequent access to the monopoly radio.

The very magnitude and horror of the November 18 carnage broke the dykes of censorship as a floodtide of already known facts forced their way into the grudging pages of the *Chronicle*, which tailed the smaller weekly *Catholic Standard* and the *Mirror*, the latter published by the main parliamentary opposition, the officially Soviet-aligned People's Progressive Party.

In addition, as the PPP's attacks on the ruling party officials of misconduct in their relations with Jonestown continued, the *Chronicle* published evidence damning to the KGB of its relations with Jonestown. It was in the foreign press that analysis of the diplomatic scene in Georgetown in relation to Jonestown was attempted.

A dispatch from Special Correspondent Gregory Ross datelined Georgetown, February 1, 1979, written by Charles A.

Krause with Gregory Ross contributing and published in the *Washington Post* of February 2, 1979 had the caption, "Guyana Exploits KGB Ties to Jonestown." The report said that both the CIA and the KGB had been very busy in the aftermath of November 18; that the Soviet press in Moscow had described the event as another example of the sickness of U.S. society and seemed set to expand the argument. "But," the article added, "that was before Guyana's prime minister L. Forbes Burnham decided that the way to dam the stream of embarrassing questions about his government's relationship with Peoples Temple was to expose links between Jonestown and the Soviet Embassy." It described Forbes Burnham as "ever the master politician." The dispatch also claimed that Mr. Burnham had visited the Soviet Union early in 1978, partly with the hope of getting financial support for development, but had received no economic support from the Soviets, "although his government was 'non-aligned' against almost all positions the United States supports".

The article said that Mr. Burnham exposed letters between Jonestown and the KGB in Guyana. The government-controlled *Chronicle* newspaper published a memo from Jonestown to Second Secretary Timofeyev of the Soviet Embassy, later identified, no doubt by the CIA at the U.S. Embassy, as a senior KGB agent. The publication did not stop the attacks from the PPP. The prime minister ordered a second secret document to be published in *The Chronicle*. The report continues, … "the government made public [sic] letters from Jonestown to the Soviet Embassy just as the suicide-murder rite began." The letter listed bank accounts with a total of $7 million and instructed that the money be withdrawn and used as the Politbureau of the Soviet communist party should decide.

In their parting generosity, the Temple leaders ignored the country that had at least offered them land and hospitality. The PPP joined the general revulsion against Jim Jones without admitting that the Soviets had blundered.

In December, 1978, the Working People's Alliance invited opposition parties to establish a group to deal with Jonestown-type issues. They agreed in Dr. Cheddi Jagan's absence from Guyana to establish The Council for National Safety (CNS) with the PPP as an active member. The CNS held two marches in Georgetown and took a delegation of members to the Commissioner of Police to question the preference enjoyed by Temple members. On Dr. Jagan's return to Guyana the PPP withdrew from the CNS on the explanation that non-socialist parties were members. The *Washington Post* dispatch, referred to earlier, claimed that Dr. Jagan had been absent on a visit to the Soviet Union. Mr. Burnham's exposure of the KGB's relations with Jonestown won him a diplomatic victory: the restraining of the main parliamentary opposition from joining with others in agitation on the Jonestown issue.

The KGB seemed to come up for mention in Guyana only in the wake of high tragedy.

For the Soviet Embassy's interfacing with Jonestown, Guyana's prime minister blew its cover to silence his Soviet-aligned opposition leader and opposite number in the political establishment. Two years after Jonestown, Dr. Walter Rodney, a much younger Guyanese luminary and rank outsider to the political-social establishment, was killed by an explosion in circumstances that pointed to the state as an accomplice in crime. There was no mention then of the KGB. Failure of the head of government to even offer condolences, or express the intention of encouraging a coroner's inquest before his own death during a final surgical operation in 1985 did not allay suspicions. A demonstration inquest under his successor did not pass muster.

A broad and pluralist international movement first spearheaded by the Guyana Human Rights Association, the Caribbean Conference of Churches, Caribbean people's movements, the Caribbean Contact Newspaper, the UK Parliamentary Human Rights Group, African American formations in many cities, organizations of many tendencies on all continents and islands, concerned academics and students and activists across the USA, students and concerned academics of all races, groups and individuals from all nations and all races and from all walks of life , the Guyanese political parties then in opposition, the Oilfield Workers Trade Union of Trinidad and Tobago, the unflinching Rodney family ,and, in 2005, the National Assembly of Guyana waged a campaign, in low gear or high gear demanding an international inquiry into Rodney's assassination.

Finally, after the PNC and the PPP governments between them had fiddled away for 33 years, the Rodney family succeeded in getting the hesitating PPP president to create a Commission of Inquiry into the unnatural death of Walter Rodney.

The Commission opened its hearings publicly in May, 2014. Robert Gates, as Clive Nobrega, former policeman, had been bodyguard to Dr. Rupert Roopnaraine, Walter Rodney's agemate and political co-worker. In his voluntary testimony to the Commission, Gates described his role in 1980 as that of a double agent. He said that he and other agents reported to a joint security committee of the security forces which was coordinated by senior police officer, Laurie Lewis. This committee had been publicly acknowledged by the PNC Government as one of its organs. Politically aware people of that period knew that the security committee, mentioned by Robert Gates, was located at Ogle Front.

Still on oath, Mr. Robert Gates said that he had been assigned the duty of deceiving and destroying an individual, and that he had deserted his post rather than carry out that duty. He further told the commission that his handler was an ex-KGB agent whom he and other agents had nick-named Brezhnev. He could not mean one out of favor with the Soviet government. Such a person would not have a Soviet passport or would not be engaged by a friendly government. He could have been a retired agent, present in Guyana with his government's knowledge, or as in the case of the CIA, a member of his country's embassy enjoying cover under diplomatic immunity.

Robert Gates's testimony reminds us of what Martin Carter knew when he wrote "After One Year" in or about 1963: Experience seems to teach that governments may come into office on a high moral note, but may have no ethical integrity; they can at any time cease to be human, and they often do. Let Martin speak on the point.

> Rude citizen! think you I do not know
> that love is stammered, hate is shouted out
> in every human city in this world?
> Men murder men, as men must murder men,
> to build their shining governments of the damned.

Chapter 14

Father Divine and Rev. Jim Jones

Interaction between the Peoples Temple and the Peace Mission

Eusi Kwayana

The relations between Father and Mother Divine's Peace Mission and the early Peoples Temple were complex. The official Jonestown website, *http://jonestown.sdsu.edu*, (Moore, n.d.), the various books on the subject, interviews with Laura Kohl and Don Beck (Jonestown survivors), and with observers located near to the Jonestown settlement agree on the fact that the majority of Jonestown members were African Americans. The finding by Jim Hougan (Hougan, 1999), a veteran and celebrated investigator, is that Jim Jones was probably a government informant before or up to 1970, and that he was retained to obtain information on the black church, in particular Father and Mother Divine's Peace Mission. Does "government" mean state intelligence institutions like the CIA or—as sometimes in the USA—the elected "branch"? Dr. Rebecca Moore, in her comment on Hougan's findings, has, if not demolished them, pointed out the need for a more convincing argument (Moore, 2009).

It is of course beyond my capacity to make such judgments. The main argument in favor of that conviction is that

COINTELPRO seemed to have left Peoples Temple outside its programs of destabilization and destruction. It is safe from this time/distance and also from Guyana not to see it as a problem to be solved now. What has struck me of the USA is that, unlike the case in the ex-colonies where I belong, CIA agents or officials, or even spies are able to admit their roles as CIA operatives or as seals without fear of public scorn. These institutions seem to be mere workplaces, whereas some of us would wince to hear that certain civilians of some note in the local community had been connected with the FBI, the CIA or the spy services, all of which seem to be regarded in the USA as everyday public service employment.

If anything, one can say fairly that Jim Jones by his own overbearing leadership and control methods invited trouble, and more so, by his own disrespect of Father Divine's Peace Mission as a separate institution of conscience—at the same time trying to borrow from it for the Peoples Temple. My own younger years' impression in Guyana of Father Divine in the USA was certainly not as a peace activist on a world scale, but merely as a charmer saying, "Peace, it's wonderful," as our press reported. We had no idea of the social range of the movement and less about its opposition to the atomic bomb and to lynching in the USA.

The literature says that Jones had an early interest in the revolution of the Peace Mission, founded by Father Divine. If Rev. Jim Jones had been a reliable narrator, in fairness to him, the experience with fathoming the Peace Mission might have been instructive, rich and enlightening. But from the written testimony of loyal Templeites, such a narrative would be risky to accept at face value.

The Peoples Temple had enough of its own resources, filled as it was with scores of talented and gifted individuals of diverse origins, especially white and black people. Jones, however, was not short on the competitive instinct and had the best in his field. Uneasy with the impression that Father Divine had made on many of his own flock, he set about removing some of the saintly mystique from his colleague. In the middle of a sermon in California after the visit to the Peace Mission, Jones called a woman who had defected from the Peace Mission to tell the audience how Father Divine had stolen into her room at night as a sexual prowler. The incident appears in the book *Six Years with God*, by Jeannie Mills as related by an early whistle blower (Mills, 1979).

Putting together the narratives of Jones's interest in Father Divine, Mother Divine and their combined work, and using all sources friendly to Jones and critical of him (the most critical being *Six Years With God*), this is the record that emerges.

As an Indianapolis-based pastor affiliated with the Disciples of Christ, Jim Jones and his assistant ministers visited the Peace Mission and were well received by one who has been called in literature an 'Incredible Messiah' and 'Dean of the Universe' in *Raven: The Untold Story of the Rev. Jim Jones and his People* (Reiterman, 1982). The author, Tim Reiterman, who traced the origins of Divine's reputed divinity to the sudden death of a judge who had sentenced Divine, said that the senior and aging Divine and Jones found common ground discussing "segregation and overpopulation." Reiterman's most important notion was that Jones sensed that Father Divine had but a short time to live. Perhaps the African-American historian John Henrik Clarke, well known for his coverage of global African history, is the most informative and instructive source of the significance of Father Divine.

In a preface to *Father Divine: Holy Husband* (Harris & Crittenden, 2011), Dr. John Henrik Clarke, constructive Pan Africanist, showed how the passing of a previous messianic figure, Rev. George Wilson Becton of Harlem, created a gap into which Father Divine moved. Clarke showed how Father Divine in Harlem had become a political force, "endorsing candidates for political office and encouraging his followers to register and vote for their own benefit and that of their community." His followers voted under such names as "Mother's Delight," "Brother of Good Faith," and "Sister who Stood by the Way." Divine did not otherwise engaged in electoral politics.

The following quotations are from Clarke's preface (Harris & Crittenden, 2011):

> "Father Divine was not a character in comic opera. Quite the contrary. He was a player in a human drama that affected the lives of millions of people, black and white. He was the product of his times and there is no way to understand him without some understanding of the interplay of the forces of human deprivation and the social dislocation that produced the atmosphere in which he thrived. He gave hope to the hopeless, and he fed the hungry and restored a sense of worth and belonging."

> "No matter what he was to the rest of the world, to the people who found new life and who lived again,

> stimulated by his presence and credos, he was real; he was father; he was God."

> "To this day few people are aware that Father Divine not only believed in but created among his followers a society based on the fundamental principle of the brotherhood of man; he gave stimulation and status to people who had nothing by involving them where their status and humanity mattered—in the human family."

Clarke recalls the Caribbean communist Claude McKay's interview with Father Divine in which Father Divine made certain declarations when asked about race, class, and cooperation with communists in anti-fascist demonstrations.

> "I have no color conception of myself. If I were representing a race or creed or color or nation, I would be limited in my conception of the universal. I would not be as I am, omnipotent."

> "I am representative of the universal through the cooperation of mind and spirit in which is reality. I cannot deviate from that fundamental. The masses and the classes must transcend the average law and accept me. And governments in time will recognize my law."

Father Divine "was ... willing to work in his own way with the Communists or any group that is fighting for international peace and emancipation of people throughout the world." He said it was not he that needed communist support and it was all right with him. Divine had apparently had the benefit of groups in Europe organizing on their own in the name of the International Peace Mission. This support was coming at a time when Europeans were starting after the scourge of the Second World War and were war weary and hungry for peace, and lasting peace. It was not the only international Peace Mission, but it was one that did not carry the risk of collaboration with the Soviet Union.

Jones had taken a bus excursion to Divine's Heaven in Philadelphia, as told by some Jonestown authors. The Peoples Temple survivors somehow do not discuss this part of the Temple story, or stress the debt of the Temple to the Rev. Major Jealous Divine. This is a pity because Jones was by no means a clone of the Peace Mission. An organization marketer, he was quick to see where similar programs would work in California, and where certain styles of management and its internal relations would make a good impression. He copied the salutation Father or Dad and applied it to himself after his acquaintance with Divine's Heaven. He also adopted the official sexual relations policy of the Heavens, in which married couples were required to abstain from sex. The pretense that this was a fundamental policy upheld by Jones in his potentially creative "apostolic socialism" is one of the main inconsistencies of the Peoples Temple. The controversy over the custody of the Stoen child and claim by Jones as his offspring from a mother outside of his marriage exposed the impunity Jones felt entitled to. It brought Jones and Jonestown into the courts of Guyana and exposed attempts to corrupt the legal system and manipulate judges. It caused an actual crisis within the state of Guyana. In a society with free media and institutions such a happening would have triggered a constitutional scandal involving many.

Justice Aubrey Bishop, to his credit, took the most principled action open to him in the circumstances by declining to proceed with the case. This decision, as he claimed, was in view of the pressures from all sides and because the judicial order had been countermanded. The Chief Justice Harold Bollers, who, though a learned judge, served his master well and had dinner with the Reverend Jones in Georgetown shortly before the case. Dr. David Dodd, sociologist and scholar in criminology, and a visitor to Guyana, was present at the meeting. Mrs. Bollers, wife of the Chief Justice, perhaps delighted in the chance for white companionship, had been on extremely friendly terms with the associates at the Temple's headquarters in Georgetown. Though hostess to Jones and company, she might not have had a clue to what was cooking.

Chapter 15

Domestic Efforts vs. Peoples Temple's

African Agricultural Traditions

Eusi Kwayana

Some have argued that Jonestown was welcomed by the ruling party in Guyana to help it push its agricultural drive. It was felt that African Guyanese people needed to get back to, or get into, agriculture and that Jonestown as an agricultural commune would set an example. However, this argument neglects the great agricultural tradition of Africans along the coasts and river banks of Guyana. Walter Rodney (Rodney, 1981) stood out among historians on Guyana as one of the very few to spend time and effort on the work done by the Africans in agriculture. The other example was Norman Cameron (Cameron, 1929), who shows their agricultural exhibitions and fairs and social infrastructure. Rodney (Rodney, 1981) went to the source of production efforts in the face of hardships in various parts of the country.

The argument is familiar that Prime Minister Burnham encouraged the Peoples Temple, led by the Rev. Jim Jones in order that his, Burnham's supporters in particular, should see the value of cultivating the land and not merely pursuing government jobs. Generally commercial jobs were largely out of their reach. If that is so, the argument is only partly true. Many educated urban people had no knowledge of the African tradition in agriculture, which was being progressively displaced by several factors, including cultural factors. It is also true that even at the high point of the decline of Africans in agriculture, large groups of Africans, mainly villagers, were keen enough to separate the ruler's rhetoric about agriculture from the reality and were heroically moving into a number of agricultural spaces with an under-supply of necessary resources.

In Guyana, as I have developed elsewhere in a forthcoming work on African village life, Africans, in the face of counter-emancipation measures by the colonial state, exploited the financial collapse of many plantations, using their collectivist culture which had brought them out of enslavement. With money earned for labor in excess of seven and a half hours a day in the post emancipation or apprenticeship regime, which they had purposefully saved, they bought numerous abandoned estates that they revolutionized into villages.

Note that they did not just "take to villages" as Dr. Cheddi Jagan wrote in *Forbidden Freedom: The Story of British Guiana* (Jagan, 1954). They bought them, as we found out from the publication of Alan Young's *Approaches to Local Self Government* (Young, 1958) and recorded in Jagan's subsequent book, *The West On Trial* (Jagan, 1966), which has a more informed commentary on the village movement.

Many interpretations have been given to these developments by historians. I myself, anxious to show Africans as something other than government workers, emphasized the agricultural and small industry aspects of their activity, well aware that when labor was in demand these populations pursued plantation labor. For many reasons I accept Rodney's classification of them as a rural proletariat, a class among which I grew up. However, the village-agricultural sector and their farming existence cannot be ignored. Briefly, almost everyone for decades after the village movement started would claim to be a farmer. Moreover, the villagers were in fact nation builders, adding an element to life on the coastland entirely different from the rest of the hemisphere.

This chapter is mainly a summary of organized group efforts from a rather recent date, in the decade of Jim Jones's arrival. In the post-emancipation decades, Africans who had been enslaved and had been forced to work as "apprentices" with their former owners after 1838, civilized the entire coastland with a new village civilization. In so doing, they made their imprint on the new institutions that developed based on free local institutions within the colonial over-lordship.

Indians from India who had been indentured as laborers on release from their contracts saw some of their numbers occupy state-prepared settlements or went and settled along river banks and established agriculture on their own. However, many African villages became multi-racial later in the 19th century because former plantation laborers from Madeira, China and India chose to settle in African villages with their own cultures and participate in the societies. This went well generally until the political disturbances of the 1960s.

African agriculture bloomed, blossomed and slowly declined. From the late sixties, a period which now concern us as the main theme of this book, its decline was gaining speed. Yet a conscious counter-movement had begun. The prime minister indeed emphasized the pursuit of agriculture. The people who needed this message most were Africans, who very readily showed up in the ranks of the unemployed. The descendants of the Indian indentured workers were still significantly tied to the land although their organizations were wisely exerting every means to get Indians better represented in teaching and in the civil service. In fact it became known only recently (the event itself occurred long ago) that Mr. J. I. Ramphal, a descendant of the indentured Indians, was the first non-white Guyanese to become head of a government department. But perceptive people could tell that the alienation of sections of the East Indian population from the land had set in from the same push and pull factors that had affected the Africans.

In the 20th century African agriculture declined more and more sharply because of the failure of the drainage systems, all of them being offshoots of the plantation drainage and irrigation system that was built with slave labor. Secondly, the crops that the majority cultivated were, except for sugarcane, highly perishable. Sugarcane lost value with time, but normally it took little time to transport it to the sugar mills. Thus, as Alan Young (Young, 1958), the first academic village historian, testified, Africans having exhausted their savings to acquire their villages and private house lots and farm lots, had no working capital left. It can be demonstrated that they did not stop there, but also developed a small scale and widespread financial sector by mobilizing small savings to sustain their enterprises. Although historians have found that African maroons introduced rice cultivation in the western hemisphere, in Guyana, which immediately concerns us, there was no continuity in this activity in general terms, but there was such activity in Essequibo and Berbice. Dr. Wazir Mohamed has scholarly writings on the forgotten role of African farmers in the rice sector.

A New Look at JONESTOWN

By the 1970s, thanks to Burnham's anxiety to solve the country's unemployment problems, he in his own way promoted farming, and some years after 1978 in fact employed some methods which critics and also loyalists claimed were in their own form in force in Jonestown.

His leader's impatience with the responses of his supporters and other Africans to produce, despite official exhortations, pushed him to coercive measures. The non-agricultural classes have little understanding of the time, the effort and, above all, the resources (like credit) that are required to achieve self-sufficiency from the land. Many think it is merely a question of one crop. What happens while the crop is maturing? If the cultivators have no alternative employment, what happens? Quite separate from the government's efforts, but seeking to meet the same demand for more agricultural activity among Africans, the African Society for Cultural Relations With Independent Africa (ASCRIA) spent many weekends actually conducting this kind of motivation. It encouraged the formation of cooperatives throughout the coastlands as well as joining with government cooperative officers in arranging education for cooperatives and for new cooperators. These were the general conditions under which new organized interest in agriculture had developed in Guyana before the coming of the Peoples Temple and the establishment of Jonestown.

The earliest of these groups known to this writer came out of East Coast and West Coast Demerara villages and they were called Young Farmers' Cooperative. Its live wire was Roy Wilson of blessed memory. I like to say with the Muslims "On whom be peace." Wilson and the Young Farmers not only pioneered a riverain[1] farm, as an idea but built their own

---

1   *Guyanese adaptation of the standard English word "riverine,"*

boat and, like the West Bank Demerara farmers recorded by Walter Rodney, plied a route between Catherine and the Georgetown where they sold their produce. At one stage Roy Wilson studied in Canada on a government cooperative scholarship through the Cooperative Union. The family 'Wilson' happened to belong to several of the most constant leaders of agricultural cooperatives located in Demerara, in Berbice, and in the Essequibo. These pioneers were well known to this writer. A co-founder of "Young Farmers' Cooperative" was Neville Jacobs, afterwards Ohene Koama.

After a Pan African Seminar organized by ASCRIA in 1970 in Georgetown, many African Americans were attracted to Guyana and to engaging in the cultivation of land and other self-help activities. This was an alternative channel of withdrawal from the USA to that which Jim Jones, then unknown in Guyana, offered to certain politically unorganized African Americans, mostly with a church background and therefore attracted to the Peoples Temple. At the same time, the Temple was formally a church and in the USA adopted a religious form and the language of religion.

The largest of the local groups were at Butenabu in the Mahaicony River Basin and the extraordinary Marudi Cooperative, which not only involved the "rural proletariat," farmers and ex-trades people, but science-minded individuals trained in physics, biology and agriculture and other disciplines, who all saw their participation as vital to a new kind of life and livelihood. One of these Marudi pioneers was Lennox Massay (see Chapter 4 for his report), who passed away in 2011 in Atlanta, to which he had returned for medical treatment.

---

which adaptation has become fully codified in the local lexicography.

My own activity with these cooperatives turned out to be misread. While still within the classification of young, I had been a close co-worker of Cheddi Jagan and a co-founder with him and his wife Janet, Martin Carter the poet, and a number of others, of the People's Progressive Party. Later Burnham and other concerned freedom seekers joined in the effort. This political history, and my explicit political interest and awareness, must have frightened Mr. Burnham, who, for some reason saw me as a rival for leadership in the society at large, since I had in June, 1971, openly criticized the drift of the Burnham-led cabinet into corruption. On International Cooperative Day in response to a request for a statement from the press, I said in part that many people in high places, including ministers of the government were making a mockery of the Cooperative Republic. In these circumstances, the government canceled the right of the thirteen land cooperatives in various parts of the country and withdrew all assistance to them from the Cooperative Department.

This short chapter may help to modify the views of those who suppose that the prime minister was justified in importing ready-made models of rural development for his constituents. So far as the Peoples Temple was concerned, its mechanical and financial resources far outmatched those available to indigenous groups. This chapter does not seek to examine the issue of one country offering sanctuary to non-nationals on mutually agreed principles publicly known and generally accepted. A private citizen, Patrick Baker, raised this issue in relation to Haitians during the aftermath of the 2010 earthquake.

This chapter serves not to discount the views scholars and others who have grappled with the complex issues of Jonestown in Guyana, but to add vital information for those readers who wish to obtain a more informed picture of the circumstances.

What is noteworthy about this political messiah Rev. Jim Jones is that he sparked hopes of salvation both in the body of followers he attracted from the USA and in the host government which expected so much from his activity. Both reaped a harvest of horrors and disappointment.

Chapter 16

A Search for Reasons

Eusi Kwayana

One aspect of the Peoples Temple's choice of, and acceptance in, Guyana has not been fully explored. It will be the basis of the political analysis offered in this chapter.

It has been expressed in many ways that the Peoples Temple from its foundation as well as in the person of its leader was "an anarchy of propensities," as one educationist says of the typical child. They were capable of various lines of development, of much life, of much death, much flexibility and much complexity. This is the political meaning from our point of view of the whole history of the Rev. Jim Jones and the means by which he rose to prominence. And he did rise to prominence and find honor as a prophet in his own country. There is eyewitness testimony in this book that elected officials in Northern California sought him out just to be photographed with him to impress their constituents. This can only testify to his standing in the community.

The concept of "an anarchy of propensities" has to be the definition of a promising, dynamic movement, offering abundant life, and ending up delivering abundant death, unless we believe, with most Faiths, that death does not matter as it is a door to a better life. The standard critique of organized religion has been that this promise has helped oppressors to pacify their victims.

Peoples Temple's settlement at Jonestown, named after the Founder/Leader Rev. Jim Jones, was in practice a state within a state. The larger state had its own supreme Founder/Leader, Mr. L. F. S. Burnham, Prime Minister and later President of Guyana.

Those who understood something of Burnham's approach to politics would reflect on the fact that a non-Guyanese was able to receive a lease of land, part of the Guyanese territory and patrimony, and to give his name to it, clearly with the full consent of the ruling party and the government it controlled. Before written evidence of how the name came to be applied came to light, many noted that there was never any official resistance or objection to the name Jonestown and that all government records and statements called it by that name. Naming of part of the country was a very jealously guarded right. The fact that Jones was able to name the Peoples Temple settlement Jonestown should signal to observers the level of intimacy and common purpose that had developed between the PNC leaders, rather than the PNC as a whole, and Rev. Jim Jones personally, rather than Peoples Temple as a whole.

A passage in a publication by the Peoples Temple's Agricultural and Medical Project (Address: P.O. Box 893, Georgetown, Guyana) titled *Jonestown, A Model of Cooperation*, (Peoples Temple, undated), a copy of which was obtained from a survivor, puts an end to all speculation about the naming.

"In October, 1974, a small group of settlers from the United States-based Peoples Temple Church came to Guyana to begin development of the Peoples Temple's Agricultural Project. They found themselves in a land of spectacular beauty, towering, graceful trees, and beautiful, friendly people of all races. Here they set about building a community that would be named Jonestown by Guyanese officials, after the founder of the Temple and initiator of the project, Bishop Jim Jones."

This excerpt from an "official" document answers Keith Scott's strong gut reservation about the project, which had impressed him when he visited it. So this name was not a result of self-promotion by Jim Jones. Then it has to be a reflection of the expectations and faith of the host government's leader.

Other cases of naming at that period in Guyana were the naming a new village, Melanie Damishana, "Melanie" after one of Burnham's daughters and "Damishana" from an Amerindian word meaning "village". The prime minister had also chosen his first name, Linden (full name: Linden Forbes Sampson Burnham), to rename an important PNC industrial and political base, Mackenzie and Wismar.

There are other cases of things and institutions named after party leaders or loyal party members like Winifred Gaskin and Ptolemy Reid. There is a health facility named after the deputy prime minister: Ptolemy Reid Rehabilitation Centre. What looks casual or ordinary to a visiting writer tells Guyanese a lot more; in this case, it warns of full acceptance and intimacy.

When Fidel Castro stopped over in Guyana in 1973 as guest of Prime Minister Burnham, Castro visited the Non-Aligned Monument on Republic Avenue. On reflection, that monument is now an historic one in view, for all practical purposes, of the forced passing from the scene of the Non-Aligned Movement, as we knew it. The monument displays the busts of the pioneers of non-alignment, Jawaharlal Nehru, Joseph Broz Tito and Kwame Nkrumah. Castro mingled with the crowd in Georgetown and later declared to the press concerning Burnham, "He has a link with the people." This was an undoubted truth, since Burnham was leader of a faction, the African faction, as against the Indian faction led by Jagan, of the once united national movement, the People's Progressive Party. In 1957 Burnham became the founder and leader of the People's National Congress, having played a strong role in the splitting of the original movement in 1955. It would be hard to find a dictator in the ex-colonies of Britain with the Westminster model that did not have "a link with the people."

1973 was the year before Dr. Walter Rodney, Guyana's international revolutionary thinker and activist, returned to Guyana from his labors in Jamaica and Tanzania. Mr. Burnham then had indeed a link with the people in the ethnically competitive situation, but had run into widespread disapproval. This was because he had created, with the help of some high achieving lawyers, including Indians, an electoral dictatorship that looked like the Westminster pattern. He was much celebrated by supporters and even by non-supporters for what they regarded as his facility with language and had a high reputation as an orator.

When Jonestown imploded on November 18, 1978, Mr. Burnham made a cryptic comment to the press. "It is an American problem," he said. In that one phrase he evoked all the well-known ghosts and played on the justified anti-U.S. feeling in most of the world, diverting attention from his own role as a facilitator, though not one with guilty knowledge.

In this cryptic remark the dictator did two things. He disclaimed all responsibility for anything that had gone wrong in Jonestown. This was perhaps his main purpose in making that remark. Quite apart from that, much more meaning can be read into that clever disclaimer depending on the observer's imagination.

The U.S. dimensions of the problem could hardly be denied. But the peculiar arrangements made between the Guyana government and the Peoples Temple, whether expressed in writing in any document or not, were well known from practice. For all practical purposes the government of Guyana was in an unequal relationship with the Rev. Jim Jones. The Guyana government, most jealous of its jurisdiction and its territorial integrity, had yielded up much of its power of oversight, including criminal oversight, to the Founder/Leader of Jonestown. For their benefit, Port Kaituma was a port of entry for a boat "Cudjoe" and another Jonestown vessel, prophetically named "The Albatross." Fully aware that a wide cross section of the people in most countries accept and expect miracles, Jones made his debut in Georgetown, Guyana, with a church service, which turned out to be a secretly intended as a healing service. Those Temple members who negotiated with the Roman Catholic authorities for the use of the Sacred Heart R. C. Church did not disclose that a healing service was intended. The R. C. Church in Guyana has not promoted healing ministries, except through praying for the sick and except when the Church itself was conducting the healing.

For example, just before the 1953 elections, the Guyana Roman Catholic Church brought to Guyana the statue of Our Lady of Fatima, a replica of the Mother of God, who had allegedly made a dramatic appearance and performed some feats of healing at Lourdes, France, which added to the mythology of the R. C. Church. Her visit to Buxton, Guyana, not separated too neatly from a local anti-communist campaign, brought down the nearest equivalent to fire and brimstone. It was an evening of thunder and lightning as the statue was paraded around the village, then known to the pro-colonial clique as "little Moscow," like Port Mourant, birthplace of Cheddi Jagan. The term also applied to Buxton and Mon Repos.

Various interests in Guyana were forced to make their own assumptions about the coming of the Peoples Temple and the establishment of an agricultural settlement. One Guyanese scholar who was off the mark with a scholarly response relatively early was Linden Lewis (Lewis, 1980). He published in the journal *Transition* an essay on Jones. In an article on the Jonestown website (htpp://Jonestown.sdsu.edu), Khaleel Mohammed (Mohammed, 2003) started a vigorous enquiry, which he allows to be mentioned in this book.

Lewis tried to explain why the Guyana government agreed to host the settlement at Jonestown. This scholar placed the government's welcome of the settlement within the context of the country's declared interest in building a socialist society. Secondly, there was great distress among sections of non-agricultural African Guyanese that Africans had been for some years increasingly alienated from the land. Many of the middle class and bureaucratic Africans attributed this tendency to the urbanization of the Africans, and at leadership level even accused them in a blanket manner of laziness. The charge of laziness is the most certain sign of alienation of these strata from the ranks of the working people and from the African experience.

No one ever recalls that just about the time when Jonestown was being offered all the facilities of the state and all encouragement, thirteen local land cooperatives had been struck off the list and their leases or permits withdrawn because they were officially considered unproductive. Those close to the activities and to those cooperatives know that the reason was fear that the cooperators were being used as training ground for a subversive army by persons, including this writer, falsely seen as rivals to the comrade leader for his post of prime minister. The forces supporting these cooperatives were in fact proactive and supportive of all round development including agriculture but also politically independent and unambitious, so far as state offices were concerned.

Khaleel Mohammed was another Guyanese academic who took an active interest in the Jonestown development. Others, apart from Linden Lewis, were faculty members of the University of Guyana. Matthews and Danns were in the Department of Sociology. Dr. Mohammed took the investigative approach, launching interviews aimed at answering outstanding questions. Although many knowledgeable individuals responded, of the 18 who responded to his public invitation, only eight eventually allowed an interview. Of these eight, four decided that their names could not be used.

Dr. Mohammed's contribution was valuable since he did not write or offer his own opinion, but sought to record and analyze a variety of opinions of people within the Guyana state or in a position to form intelligent opinions about government policy.

The burden of responses available to Mohammed places the Jonestown connection in an ideological as well as an ethnic context. The citizens were of the opinion that as a socialist, once a program of settlement in the jungle appealed to the Burnham government, which had proclaimed socialist intentions, he (Burnham) would naturally embrace the project. Their understanding was that here was a struggling "socialist" third-world government without the necessary money to develop the interior. Jones with his willing band of followers, a work discipline, and a willingness to inhabit the jungle was a welcome model and example. At the end of his report, Dr. Mohammed was still hopeful that persons with real knowledge of aspects of Jonestown would be emboldened enough to speak out.

Dr. Mohammed's experience throws some light on how a dictatorship affects various strata of its citizens. The great state of mind affecting most citizens outside of the corridors of power was fear of being accused of disloyalty to the party and government.

It is an important paper because it shows the state of consciousness of those who understandably judge the regime by its public statements. Others of us knew by experience that those engaged in politics and the political process were aware of the gap between policy declaration and policy implementation and the element of posturing.

Any supposition that Jonestown was the result of a considered defence strategy of the Guyana government was answered recently in the following passage in a publication, 27 years after Jonestown. It is written by retired Brigadier David Granger (Granger, 2005, p. 44):

> "The bizarre mass-suicide of the Peoples Temple sect at Jonestown, in the Barima-Waini Region, on November 18, 1978, focused unfavorably global attention on Guyana. The sect had been allowed to settle in the hinterland as a part of the government's general policy of occupying the Essequibo territory claimed by Venezuela. The settlement was entirely a political decision, although it may have been taken as part of the general defence posture. When news broke of the massacre, however, the Guyana Defence Force (GDF) was caught totally by surprise. It had to mount a hasty operation with the grisly mission of helping the U.S. army to remove nine hundred decaying corpses of the sect's members who had allegedly died from poisoning. The Jonestown massacre clearly showed that defence policy-making entirely in civilian hands, was not being coordinated between the Administration and the Defence Force on important issues which could have strategic repercussions for Guyana's strategic integrity."

The comment above is the first known free speech in print of a high military officer active in the GDF during the Jonestown developments. The author was trained in Guyana, Britain, Brazil and Nigeria and was between 1979 and 1990 Commander of the Guyana Defence Force, in the last years under Chief of Staff, ex-policeman, Norman McLean. From 1990 to 1992 he was adviser on national security to Guyana's President Desmond Hoyte.

There is a popular and reasonable view, shared also by Jim Jones in his wide ranging commune addresses, that Burnham wanted the settlement of U.S. citizens in that location as a deterrent to attacks by Venezuela, which, by occupying Ankoko Island, had given evidence of its disposition to use force to support its territorial claims against the emerging republic. Granger's comment does not deny this view. It says on high military authority that this important strategic decision was taken exclusively at the level of the Commander in Chief, Prime Minister L. F. S. Burnham and was not part of a territorial security plan coordinated with the military.

The GDF boasted one of the several security intelligence organizations maintained by the PNC government, others being the Police Special Branch, and the National Service Intelligence. If there was this kind of decision taken by a kitchen cabinet, there could also be other decisions and understandings involving the Peoples Temple and its roles in Guyana. Most of the PNC people who can speak with authority on these matters are very likely no longer with us.

Former public servants and political survivors still silence themselves by public service rules or political loyalty or by fear of reprisals. In fact the public service disclosure rules were intended to apply to lawful business. Only one of the PNC leaders of those days remains in public life and may have little time for defending Jonestown.

Those who don't accept the political perceptions of the alliance between those two forces (the Peoples Temple and the PNC) and seek concrete evidence must await the chance revelation as often happens of this evidence. In my own investigations, state operatives of that period have said that documentary evidence such as existed was destroyed in the fire to the Office of the General Secretary, People's National Congress and Ministry of National Development building in 1979. But there is other evidence.

Some of it is scrappy and circumstantial but persuasive. After the Declaration of Sophia in December 1974, read out on the radio by the prime minister, the nation was forewarned. The PPP was uneasy, feeling that it was being outdone in the way its opposite number followed up rhetoric with action, both on penetration more strategic than developmental. In the Declaration of Sophia the prime minister proclaimed the doctrine of the Paramountcy of the party over the state. In this multi-party, multi-racial, and multi-ethnic small country, Guyana became, as it is now, in all respects except the membership of parliament and the national assembly, a one-party state. Moreover, the doctrine was to be imposed on the state by administrative means and without legislation.

The leader had proclaimed the introduction of Executive Secretaries, but stopped short of placing these or providing for these in the annual estimates of revenue and expenditure. Perhaps it was with Peoples Temple and many other non-traditional activities in mind that the Ministry of National Development was re-invented as Office of the General Secretary, People's National Congress and Ministry of National Development. Its estimates took a peculiar format in the Annual Estimates of Revenue and Expenditure. Generally, after the provisions for the civil (public) service establishment, each area of expenditure would be listed, with as much detail as possible with sub-heads of the item for the purpose of financial control.

Non-substantial or minor items of the Estimate were grouped under the heading "Other Charges," which always carried its own details and listing, all of them specific or by category. e.g., fuel charges. An inspiration caused me to seek an explanation of the 1975 Estimates when the Ministry of National Development was duly included without its prefix "Office of the General Secretary, PNC," which appeared on the signboard of the Ministry. There in the official estimates stood the sub-head "Other Charges," $10 million, a large figure in those years with not a single detail. One woman senior public servant smilingly explained in answer to my question about the absence of details, "This is a ministry with a difference."

This "ministry with a difference" was the center of relations between the official government and the Peoples Temple's development project at Jonestown.

Chapter 17

Race and Gender in the Peoples Temple

Eusi Kwayana

Race and gender are the outstanding issues that revolutions and revolutionary movements to date have not been able to solve. Race has received far more attention, perhaps because it involves more outsiders than gender does. All this does not mean that race has been blessed with anything like a solution. The historical influence of imperialism is shown in the fact that dark skin is still the wrong skin, having to be accommodated, and made the subject of special provisions. Women were a majority both in the Peoples Temple in the USA and in Jonestown, Guyana, and a majority of these women were African Americans, as stated in Rebecca Moore's *The Demographics of Jonestown* (Moore, R. (n.d.) on the Alternative Considerations of Jonestown ... web site:

> "Almost twice as many females as males lived in Jonestown, which becomes significant when we look at the leadership patterns in the community. Black females made up the largest group of residents of Jonestown (45%), with white females comprising 13%. Black males made up over one-fifth (23%) with white

males making up a tenth and the remainder falling in the Mixed or Other categories. Clearly women played an important role in the community, both numerically and organizationally."

In reviewing a book on Peoples Temple by the African-American scholar C. Eric Lincoln, who looked at the Peoples Temple as Black Religion, Moore comments that Peoples Temple lacked a womanist perspective. "Womanist" is the term many African-American women prefer to "feminist," which they often consider to be too gender separatist. The all-round assault on black males in the USA has conditioned African-American women into a sense of solidarity with the male that is not always appreciated by successful males, or is simply seen as a duty.

Readers should be in no mystery about the practical sexuality, which is well distributed among all known faiths as it is in all human institutions. Not every practitioner or every house of worship however has tarnished itself with exploitative sex. *In Sex in the City* ... (Kohl, n.d.), Laura Kohl writes with such detachment and sincerity it is easy to see why the role played by either church or commune is neither strange nor unique.

The modern and enlightened attitude to sex, as I understand it, is that sex is permissible and not to be criminalized provided it takes place between consenting parties. This essay will use that standard, provided the consent itself is knowable and provided power relations are not an issue. What is the quality or standard of consent when the woman feels constrained by status or tradition? I would suspect any consent between employer and employee or in any similar relationship, unless the parties plan marriage in any agreed form.

Jim Jones began his ministry with the complex of a person set apart, for which, who can blame him? He then developed the complex of a champion, of a prophet and then of a prophet pastor. This was a short step to the complexes of a Messiah. James Garrett (see his article, Chapter 08, "Context for Leo Ryan's Involvement with Jonestown"), a former minister in the Black Panther Party, has explained that some male leaders of the Panthers in many cases exploited the Panther sisters using their authority so that an organization of public revolution became in part an organization of private domination and ravishment. The Black Panthers had a rich and humanistic history of service to the poor, of the will both to affirm and defend race and to overcome it, of proclaiming the right of the black and poor to self-defence. Yet it stumbled, as human society as a whole has done on the gender issue. It could have a woman leader, Chairperson Elaine Browne, without loss of sexist attitudes of the under developed males.

Jim Jones had married normally and at an age which signified an interest in at least an attempt at a stable life. Citing of names will be beyond the purposes of this article and will serve no useful purpose other than repetition of gossip, since these relationships have been established already by competent writers. It will therefore deal with the sexual praxis of the Peoples Temple and especially of Jim Jones, its Prophet.

In his public sessions most of which were mainly harangues, with a minority of them being seriously focused, Jones exercised the maximum freedom. As his authority increased and his control became more and more absolute, his range of communication became more liberated and also more slanderous. If in San Francisco, because of the encircling society, Jones exercised some restraint in his lectures, he had no such constraint in Guyana and enjoyed total freedom. In Guyana there was no media that could expose him: he was in full control of truth. He embodied the media. Like the House of Israel, he enjoyed the use of the state-owned radio station Guyana Broadcasting Corporation (GBC), later a monopoly spanning two regimes, the PNC and the succeeding PPP after 1992. The People's Progressive Party, the main parliamentary opposition after two and a half decades of exclusion from office, won elections in 1992 with the pledge to establish democracy. As this is being written, two decades later, the media situation is of a different format. The government radio monopoly remained intact during the first ten years of the new People's Progressive Party/Civic (PPP/C) administration. It then gave way under pressure from domestic and regional civic protest. Though it was a system established by law, it was seen by public opinion outside of government and its supporters as highly discriminatory and unfair. Now, print media operators are free to operate at their own risk.

One amazing feature of Jones's practice was that he corruptly over-presented sex as mere physical activity, like drinking or eating, when in fact it is not and has consequences of a physical, emotional, social, communal, and public health nature. The way it is conceived and practiced has large impacts on friendship, respect, dignity, and human development. No wonder social and political activists as far apart as Lenin and Gandhi were concerned about its abuse. Not surprisingly they both held the dignity of women high. Lenin elevated the struggle to the domestic sphere by declaring "There is no woman's work." Gandhi wrote with clarity and conviction about women's equality. It should not surprise readers that Jones invoked the names of both Lenin and Mahatma Gandhi. Kemetic or Egyptian philosophy recognized the significance of gender as an innate polarity, but Jones was not informed on those matters.

In a certain sense, the experience of Christine Miller, both African American and woman suggests that that sample of society represented by Jonestown would rather support a sick patriarchy than give a hearing to a warning from a black woman, although she was the voice of sanity. Somehow I have the feeling that if women like Laura Kohl, Nana Culley (matriarch of Buxton, Guyana), Caroline Bourne, (a Garveyite of Kitty, prominent in resistance to the 1948 shooting of Indian sugar workers of Enmore), Emma Barnes (of Buxton), and Annie Wright (of early Campbellville, Georgetown, and a PPP Jaganite pioneer, later PNC), to say nothing of Gertrude Allsopp (market woman and a PNC stalwart of Georgetown) — if at least three of them were around, they would have taken matters in hand and overpowered the fast talking tyrant. They have done this often in Guyana's history when the petty tyrant is not armed.

Nana Culley locked the door of the village office against a village overseer, considered out of order. Church women at Beterverwagting, Guyana, took down the stairs of a church minister to stem his authority. Womanist power is rather repressed when the tyrants come armed with weapons or with any class of enforcers.

All the survivors whom I interviewed and all of those who have written about Peoples Temple have readily admitted Jones's deception and manipulation.

This is how it is that Jones at least by a sizable number of Templeites was regarded as a political or revolutionary leader and not as a spiritual Messiah. Few self-respecting people will allow a religious leader to proclaim his sexual virility and to name names of people with whom he had slept, or so he claimed, always, as Templeite Laura Kohl noted with irony, at great sacrifice to himself and always for him very reluctantly and for the good of the movement. Jones boasted of how desired he was by women. He talked of a congressman's relative who could afford to make a large donation to the Temple, but only if he slept with her and how he obliged for the sake of God's work, that is the work of Jim Jones.

His technique in winning bodies seemed to be to present a picture of boundless energy to promote himself as a healer, and also as one capable of bringing about social change and end discrimination, as a person who could abolish hunger and homelessness, heal the sick and deliver real social goods, like education and healthcare. This, apart from his own reported personal attractiveness, made him a superstar, a man larger than life with whom it would be an honor to associate in bed. Those who desired him would perhaps choose the aspect of him that they most admired.

He had taken his son, very young, Stephan, one night on a visit to his own mistress, confusing the young boy beyond reason. The boy knew that his father was betraying his mother in a major way, showering love on a mistress that he did not shower on his mate, his wife, the child's mother. In his recklessness he demoralized both wife and son, and Jones had to stage sudden acute illness to move his devoted wife Marceline to rush to his side.

His sexual activity impinged on the governance of Jonestown. Writers who have been studying Jonestown and the website materials claim that ultimately it was Jim Jones with a narrow circle of white women who ran Jonestown. This small band would therefore have great influence with him. The Planning Commission was one thing, as explained on the organization chart, which even to some friends was another of Jones's public relations cards.

Christine Miller
Photo Courtesy of California Historical Society, MSP 3800

Had the most trusted advisers not been bed intimates of Jones and loyal and devoted to him, being under his spell, then a number of influential colleagues, men or women, might have swung White Night proceedings away from the apocalypse. Christine Miller stood up to Jim Jones and Marceline Jones, who took a rather different position. A more detached team of advisers, not amorously connected to Jones with sexual intimacy might have saved the whole collapse of Jonestown. Decisions of a collective or of any organization serving a social purpose ought not to be bedroom affairs. Even where sex is not an issue, decisions about public matters become unreal when taken by a small ring locked in intimacy. If Laura Kohl and

Stephan Jones had been present with Miller at Jonestown on November 18, 1978, there would be the possibility of a strong resistance to Jones's decree. Change in the regime would have been a likelihood.

An example is the extent to which Christine Miller came forward and challenged Jones's theory of the need for suicide on the final White Night and the wisdom and compassion which poured from her as she did it.

Christine Miller is, on careful analysis, not a casual casualty of Jonestown but the true heroine, the typical soul of all the aspirations of Peoples Temple and Jonestown. She was the ideal revolutionary. She was involved, she was loyal, and she shared the hopes and aspirations. Moreover, she was critical and did not let some fanciful dream or infatuation cloud her critical faculty. She was a working class woman from the cotton fields.

According to writings on her provided by the Jonestown Institute on the Alternative Considerations of Jonestown website (http://jonestown.sdsu.edu/), she was not a new comer to the Temple. Yet, an examination of the membership of the Jonestown Planning Commission does not show her listed as a member of that Commission. If the information is accurate, it is to be wondered how such a striking humanity could be left out of the Planning Commission, which according to Beck (Jonestown member), was supposed to handle "emergencies" but apparently had not met, or had time to meet, on the emergency of emergencies.

The details are lurid and can be read on the Alternative Considerations of Jonestown website (http://jonestown.sdsu.edu/)

A New Look at JONESTOWN

and in some books. It is on these that this writing is founded. In fact the source most used is the speeches of the Rev. Jim Jones himself. In fairness to him, however, we should examine his claim that his sexual adventures were undertaken for the sake of the cause.

Many U.S. citizens reading these opinions will perhaps place the writer among the non-liberals or perhaps the religious — or irreligious — Right, because as a practicing revolutionary from the Caribbean he is aware that news of sexual excesses on the part of leaders brings out the worst authoritarian features of the old politics.

These circumstances invite comment on the political compulsions of Jim Jones, which for him were to an extraordinary degree bundled with his sexual ambitions. It is quite possible that under the pressure of closely working together in a small space, affection can spring up between a superior and a subordinate. The law at present looks with displeasure on advances from a higher official to one lower down on the administrative chart, and sexual harassment is a well-established offence, though committed in the most exalted positions of the state such as the military forces. Tailhook[1] is a monument to what insecure young women may suffer in disciplined organizations. If higher officials are allowed with all their credentials of power and right to dispose of others on this basis, we can say goodbye to thoughts of a new society.

This passage from the writings of Laura Kohl (Kohl, n.d.), a loyal Templeite, should be read with Christine Miller in mind

---

1 *Refers to the allegations of mass sexual assault by the U.S. military at the 35the Annual Tailhook Association Symposium in 1991 in Las Vegas, Nevada.*

and her gentle, single, unpopular, jeered and therefore heroic opposition to Jim Jones's suicide decree on November 18, 1978.

> "I could tell that he was a sexual being. As time went on, Jim spoke about members–both men and women– who were about to stray, and how he had helped keep them in the fold by making a personal sacrifice and having sex with them. He would often let on the identities of these people, but he always made it known that he hadn't enjoyed the sexual contact and that he had only altruistic reasons for doing it. Of course, if they were attractive he would make the 'sacrifice' sooner rather than later."

Christine Miller's defiance redeems Temple womanhood.

Chapter 18

Jones's Revolutionary Praxis

Eusi Kwayana

Although I hoped to write a new kind of book on Jonestown, in part on the Peoples Temple and on the Rev. Jim Jones himself, I had not intended at the start to reconstruct his stated beliefs and political-religious philosophy. This has now become an objective because, as a political activist and a critic of political praxis, I have been reading some of his available sermons, or pulpit conversations. Ignoring his own testimony, which is what these materials are, seems to me most unfair and a vital omission. The official Jonestown website at San Diego State University (SDSU), Alternative Considerations of Jonestown (http://jonestown.sdsu.edu [Moore, n.d.]), was the source of welcome information from his recorded tapes.

The book I intended to put together was an examination of Jonestown from a Guyanese viewpoint. This is still my purpose.

The mass "revolutionary suicide" as Jones presented it, or mass murder, or mixture of suicide and murder, which took place in Jonestown, Guyana, on November 18, 1978, remains a stain on the name not only of Guyana but also of Jim Jones. From his early life, Jim Jones showed or professed a real interest in religion and in major social change. What he turned out to be, and the harvest he reaped, will therefore reflect on other persons and other movements using the same language, stances and slogans.

He had an extraordinary odyssey, from faith to faith, and institution to institution, and eventually felt that he had struck the right mixture of what he had sampled. He was inspired by larger-than-life figures; he identified with them and determined to be one or more of them. Unlike most boys or girls in maturing years, he never lost those ambitions—or more accurately, aspirations. They were noble in themselves, but Jones never quite developed the mastery of self that is required to sustain the roles he felt called upon to play.

There is impressive evidence, if not convincing fact and inference, taken from Jones's physical and social migrations to suggest that Jones was some kind of political instrument, a wheeler and dealer, perhaps someone charged by a paymaster with a great, if horrific, enterprise. People who take on such institutions or assignments are not usually persons with ideals or persons who wish to cherish and be associated with ideals.

Such persons fall in with the vision of the English poet[1]:

> These, in the day when heaven was falling,
> The hour when earth's foundations fled
> Followed their mercenary calling
> And took their wages and are dead.

---

1   *Quoted from E.A. Houseman's poem Number XXXVII, Epitaph on an Army of Mercenaries, in "Last Poems" (1922).*

There is something in the Eurocentric portrait that does not fit Jones. In order to understand Jonestown we must get at his clock and its mechanism, that is, what made him tick. Yet we can venture at this early stage to say that had he lived, it would not be difficult to convict him of a capital offence, the evidence being so plentifully available. It will be necessary to isolate the "many men in one man" and then to reassemble them again to compose the segmented and complex personality. He could be charged with counseling the felony of suicide and perhaps more direct forms of homicide, that is, infanticide. He could be an accessory before the fact of the numerous crimes.

Yet after 35 years, there is no evidence of Jones having converted the assets of the Peoples Temple to his own use. If he himself was an instrument of the CIA, then he was the most conflicted person alive. A mind control experiment could be carried out as easily in one of the California locations, where some high degree of mind control over the majority was in fact achieved, as in Jonestown.

In California, there could be a combined operation with the FBI and the CIA or COINTELPRO or dozens of other agencies. And so what? Is it seriously contended that the supposed principals of the mind control experiment would be satisfied only with the final outcome and not with clinical evaluations as months or half-years passed by.

At the same time, there is clear evidence that some members of the Peoples Temple had come from all kinds of suspect backgrounds, including working for intelligence agencies. As examples, at least one woman, Edith Roller, the diarist, and one man, Mike Prokes, had made these admissions.

Those who see Jonestown as a CIA creation would have to find a motive for Jones's apparently selfless service to the CIA. The only suspicion available of Jones's use of funds, apparently of no credible origin, was his ability to afford a stay of three years in Brazil with his family. The authors of *Raven* (Tim Reiterman and John Jacobs, 1982) have revealed that this stay was at the expense of Peoples Temple. This caused me to question privately whether Peoples Temple had not been over indulgent.

Dr. Rebecca Moore's showing of the film *Jonestown: The Life and Death of Peoples Temple* (Nelson, 2006) at SDSU around midyear 2006 allowed me to meet and later to interview a number of survivors of Jonestown, whose testimony is included in this book and precedes this chapter.

These interviews were mainly with survivors who remained loyal to the vision of Peoples Temple and, as some of them saw it, the host government of Guyana. They could not help me much with the relations between the two governments, that of Peoples Temple and that of Guyana, host to Peoples Temple. In the press conference held by the then Minister of Information after Jonestown, on November 21, 1978, she rejected my proposition that Jonestown was a state within a state. She said, "No, it was not a state within a state. It was a farm." Her reply appeared the next day in *Dayclean* (see Chapter 11 for full report), a political newsletter that I represented.

However, the survivors were very helpful in their description of the internal politics of the internal state, Jonestown. It is impossible to make sense of Jonestown without making sense of the internal politics of the Peoples Temple. In this sense, Jonestown must be seen as an extension of the Temple or as a new birth, or even a fulfillment of it. In the San Francisco church at one stage, members described Jonestown as the "mission field," a term that needs examination.

Non-white peoples have been assumed to need "missionaries" and that is where the "mission field" idea comes from. The term plays up to church members, but does not fit in with Jones's studied political correctness. The idea of a "mission field" in a developing country may have appealed not only to the Christians in Peoples Temple, but to certain types of donors.

The internal politics of Peoples Temple was made up of its institutions and their interactions, the interaction of the individual members and groups of members, the effects of the outside world on the membership, and all of these with the ultimate leader. This last element led to political creativity on the part of the Temple and more accurately on the part of Rev. Jim Jones.

For the time being, it can be said that the institutions of the Peoples Temple were:

- The Rev Jim Jones, Pastor and Prophet
- The secretaries and officials who formed an orbit immediately around him, that is, the inner circle
- The Planning Commission
- The general assembly
- The communion service or open meal
- The healing services, a version of the general assembly
- Jim Jones's sermons or discourses
- Relations with the Guyana government
- Jones's bilateral and opportunistic links with one or another member

It should not surprise anyone that Rev. Jim Jones's standards bore the influence of the rather deformed political culture in which he was raised. What may surprise observers is that Temple people of clear idealism and positive standards could excuse his wiles and wiliness on the ground that "after all, Jim was doing the right thing," meaning politically. We all have to learn that leaders or messiahs are humans and will carry over into their liberation work the same complexes that helped or haunted them as persons.

This came out most clearly in a reported letter to Jim Jones by the Gang of Eight at Peoples Temple in San Francisco. According to the SDSU Jonestown website (Moore, n.d.), young men complained in writing to the Leader about "the staff" and its excesses, mainly sexual. They seemed very well informed on the sexual politics of Peoples Temple and with its implications. They made direct accusations of the leader himself, but with generous forgiveness in the same breath. They also pledged their allegiance to him despite his known adventures. This attitude was not confined to young people. It engulfed the entire membership. There is no better way [sexual favors] yet invented of spoiling leaders.

Jones claimed to be the reincarnation of a number of historical figures. Although he had affirmed kinship or succession to a number of purely spiritual figures, his real model, considered achievable, was Lenin, who had been the dominant figure in laying the theoretical base for the October Revolution of 1917.

It may be useful to study a typical discourse based on the Jonestown SDSU site's transcript of tape number Q242 (Moore, n.d.). It is a prolonged pep talk, which allowed the leader and teacher to move from topic to topic, issue to issue. The issues are most mixed and rich in variety.

The tape starts with comment on the quality of a delegation of the Young Socialist Movement (YSM), the youth arm then of the ruling PNC. It is a night session at Jonestown. He tells his flock that the YSM delegation, as he judged from their responses, approved of atheism. He excused the late start of the meeting by explaining "but we have some important people here." He asked his audience to understand that from his conversation with the YSM delegation he was encouraged in many respects. Rev. Jones's glee at discovering the alleged atheists was remarkable.

He commended the silent guests for their advanced ideological development. He let them know that Jonestown also had many of the atheist breed. Next, he told the Jonestown residents and communards that the Guyana government carries out a heavy mandate of indoctrination in socialism in all departments. "Heavy mandates come, heavy indoctrination," he assured his congregation.

He next told the audience, the mass assembly, that when he talked of a political party he had only one party in mind. But when asked by somebody which Party he meant, he replies, "I mean PNC. I am not asking about any other kind of goddamn party, I said, 'which is our Party?'"

He advised them that they ought to know what party is theirs when asked. He advised that if he, Jones himself, came up with the person and asked the question, they should feel free to endorse the Party in question. Without hesitation, it is clear that Jones is instructing his followers in devious public relations. He could hardly be doing this in the presence of the YSM delegation, so the words he uses are often not what he intends. This happens in all of Jim Jones's speeches. We would understand by "we have some important people here" that the delegation was still present. Yet, he says in their presence that Temple's endorsement cannot be trusted. His advice implies the relations with the PNC are cozy and known and accepted by both to be cozy; that they are linked against all others.

However, in Guyana, these YSM stalwarts would not tell any crowd that they were atheists. If Jones is truthful, then he is misreading the popular culture of Guyana. He understood it better when he made his debut with healing services. The majority of Guyanese of any faith will not discount a real miracle of healing. Here we have an example of Jones taking upon himself to make the particular members of the YSM accountable to a foreign crowd when they are not accountable to that extent to their own fellow Guyanese. Using the confidence of the YSM delegates, Jones announced to the crowd that in the Guyana government departments, officials were indoctrinated under "heavy mandates" that extended even to schools. This YSM admission was the substance of heavy attacks on the PNC government by Human Rights forces and anti-dictatorial organizations and parties.

Jones is preoccupied with suspected attempts of the Concerned Relatives, an organization in the USA reported to be made up of some relatives of Jonestown residents and wanting to disrupt the Jonestown community. On his own testimony, he also takes advice from the YSM delegates to be on the alert for CIA operatives in their midst. According to Jones, one YSM man advised him to "get guns" as the CIA would certainly send people there to kill him. Jones told the crowd all of this in the presence of the YSM delegation.

For the moment, although this mood is not constant in all his discourses, Jones is impressed with the PNC. The crowd must let them know that they are "our party." He welcomes what the YSM calls the "indoctrination," happy about the advice that Jonestown should arm against attempts, almost certain, of the CIA to remove them.

He repeats that a YSM woman had told him that she "wished him God's blessing and prayers," and said to Jones that people should be grateful for what he had done. The woman was probably distinguishing herself from the alleged professing atheists.

Another welcome aspect of the Guyana government's policy was its policy on extradition, a process allowing a foreign country to apply for the right to take into custody a suspect who is physically in the jurisdiction of another government.

Jones praised the PNC for not having such provisions in its law, which may have endangered some members of Peoples Temple in Jonestown. "No matter what crime we've committed, Guyana makes no such agreement like that," he assured the gathering. Guyana won high praise for not having any such agreements with foreign countries. As a keen observer of governmental behavior, Jones must have known that in February 1970, at the Seminar of Pan Africanists and Black Revolutionary Activists organized by ASCRIA in Georgetown, Prime Minister Burnham, who by invitation declared the seminar open, had in his speech offered sanctuary to freedom fighters from Africa. On a question from the floor by Jitu

Weusi, an African American, Mr. Burnham followed up by saying that the same sanctuary was open to freedom fighters from the USA. This diplomatic victory of the popular forces in the USA was later to serve Peoples Temple's interest.

Jones then went off to discuss and grill his hearers on the assassination of Martin Luther King, Jr., testing their knowledge of the investigation and the inconsistencies in it. He noted the fate of a woman who believed that she was a witness to the assassination and who was sent by the authorities to a mental hospital.

Switching once again, he attempts to quote the exemplary YSM. This is how he renders it.

> "Now this Young Socialist Movement man, he wanted us to do all we could to get more security. He said we needed to get guns. He said the CIA will come here and try to kill you, yes, you. They'll try to kill Jim Jones. We said we had had ... well, he said why aren't you people doing more about it, and you are not alert enough. He said look up. He said, I'd look up. You can smile; look up at everybody that comes in here."

The Guyanese expression would be "look out," that is, "be alert."

He next reported that he found more morale boosting from a Guyanese public servant.

> "The guy from the Ministry of Energy called it a socialist what? Socialist utopia? I had to talk to him a long time. It was important to get the understanding

> across to him, that's why the delay. But if they can see it how much more should we see it? If you have managed to get this movement here without some CIA agent in it, I'll be mightily surprised. It takes a person of genius, and you have that. If you been able to get somebody here that's not in the CIA I'll be mightily surprised."

Jones used this commendation to urge his followers to report everything.

> "When you hear gossip, report it. When you hear it and don't report it, or you see somebody doing something strange or negative or violating rules and don't report it, [you] may be helping a murderer. You may be helping someone that may later be a participant."

He works this theme for a few seconds, warns about "those who would try many romances" and "changing buddies." This leads him to warn against asking questions about Venezuela. (At the time there was no Bolivarian socialism in Venezuela.)

> "These questions make us all nervous. What we ought to do is turn you loose on the border and we wouldn't have no problem with you. If you want to go to Venezuela make application tonight and we will get you on the path headed for Venezuela. Put your application, when the time is we'll let you go. Cause if you going to Venezuela, I'm confident, you ain't going to get back to the USA alive."

The session then proceeds into a kind of film review. It is a method used by Jones, who had some teaching experience, for sharpening the global political understanding of the members. He would prescribe a film to be exhibited. For some films, viewing was mandatory for members, and from the dialogue, it would seem that he reserved the right to grant waivers to members who claimed to be wanted for duty. On the occasion of this discussion, a member had excused herself on the explanation that she had been working at the bakery. He said that he did not recall issuing any waiver for that film. The reader could easily recall Lenin's advice, "Every cook has to learn how to govern." The Father, as he had begun to style himself after a visit to Father Divine's Heaven, did not shrink from micro-management.

Anyone claiming that the Jonestown membership had no chance to participate in public discussion would have to explain these meetings, often running for hours, as well as their place in decision making. It is also vital to establish their true nature in an evaluation of Jonestown egalitarianism. Of course, they were neither properly planned discussions, nor discussions conducted in a style that encouraged maximum participation.

The film then under discussion was *The Parallax View* (Pakula, 1974). It deals with the assassination of a senator. It was shown long before there was any notion that a senator would visit them. The film, therefore, was not chosen with the visit of U.S. Congressman Ryan in mind. During the sessions too, helpers recorded highlights and conclusions on black boards to improve the teaching quality of the sessions. Jones would offer his own explanations of the political and personal behavior experienced in the film and would do so without the use of high-sounding jargon.

This and other films provided a chance for practicing detective work, character analysis and other features of general knowledge which would be useful for a community with the Peoples Temple's aspirations. The issue will always be whether there was freedom of speech and who took the decisions. These processes greatly impressed visitors, including the officials of the USSR. Indeed, Feodor Timofeyev, the resident consular and the chief of the press department of the Embassy of the USSR in Georgetown, praised Jonestown as "the first socialist and communist community of the United States of America, in Guyana and in the world."

Most of the gathering usually responded to Jones's questions or pauses with shouts of approval, with applause, high or low, and only a few individuals ever spoke in their own right. However, he would commend correct answers and deplore the failure of many to grasp the essential points.

Jones often demonstrated his ethics or his opinion of proper political attitudes from incidents or remarks during his sessions with the members.

Part of the sessions was given over to world news, the progress of the revolution around the world, its victories and reverses. Brief analysis would follow.

The discussion does not move on with any planned sequence. The sequence emerges at the end when we can look back at it. In one passage, Jones is talking about a man he has had to convince that Jones and others were not the CIA. He did this by showing the actions of the CIA against black leaders in the USA. He thought he had turned an unfriendly man into a friendly person.

> "He walked with me all the way down to the point. He said to me, look, I want to know about if they're going to take care of your internal security. He could 'a been a spy doing that, but he wasn't. I said, yes, it had been taken care of, 'cause they are licensing personal bodyguards with a very, very heavy piece of equipment. But you don't need to talk about that. The government is doing that for us. We don't have any weapons, and we don't have right now, and we don't have at all. Right?"

Catching him on the run, Jim Jones described a very dramatic and significant incident.

> "And I'm not talking about ... he's a very good worker here. But today, I, I'd walked till hell froze over before any of you'd give me water. And my vocal cords are so sore, I asked for water twice before I got water. I should not have ask for water."

The audience responded, "Right!"

> "The goddamn water. And then, a black woman go to get it. I said, don't given me no goddamn water. I don't want no black Shanda James [a Jonestown resident] going. I said, get that water out of her hand. You white people on that committee enough to have enough sense to grab that shit without telling you that. What the hell do you think they 'da thought of me if a black young woman would hold my water and I take the damn water and drink. Hmm?"

Pause.

"You gonna watch appearances if you're a socialist."

As part of this session, Jones again stressed the need to regard the People's National Congress as the members' preferred party in Guyana. There was a very practical reason for this, since it was the governing party, with no prospect of change then in sight. Yet Jones was proposing this or rather insisting on it as political tactics. At other times he clearly favored the positions and rhetoric of the People's Progressive Party (PPP), the one since 1969 officially affiliated to the Communist and Workers' Parties in Moscow. Shortly before the 1978 visit of the Concerned Relatives, an oppositional force to Jim Jones, he had assured the gathering that the PPP had given strong solidarity to Jonestown and the Temple against the interference of U.S. Congressman Leo Ryan.

Having made it clear that the residents embraced the PNC, and after requiring individuals to take the same position, Jones had to arm them with answers regarding the internationally profiled PPP. He quoted a PNC woman leader as saying that the PNC was the vanguard, a phrase not popular to Jonestown residents. Perhaps the Communist Party, USA, was too realistic to deem itself the vanguard there. If challenged or questioned, they were to say that the PNC was the vanguard. He said that often the PNC "will not knock the PPP." Neither should the Jonestown people "knock the PPP." Yet if they were asked why they preferred the PNC their answer should take this form: "I don't like the PPP policy of *aapan jaat*." He explained that the Hindi phrase meant "vote for your own kind."

Jones added:

"From what I have studied of the history of both sides, they have appealed to race on one occasion by *aapan jaat*, telling the East Indians to vote their own kind. That's a terribly backward thing for a Marxist to do. Why, even human geneticists know that we're all one kind. Right?"

What conclusion may be drawn from the foregoing?

Social change or revolution in the 20th and 21st centuries, if it is to take root in simple, sublime, social justice and humanist base, may not avoid strong egos. But the movement will fail if it entertains cult leaders. On the other hand, who is anyone to deny others by divine prescription a place or a role in the human need for social change? Jim Jones, like Father Divine, chose the committed or enchanted following rather than the open society to conduct his revolution. Divine reigned like an earthly deity and intervened in the world society against war and the atom bomb and against lynching in the USA. He astonished his angels (followers) by dying peacefully, leaving them to their own devices.

Jim Jones did not take the chance of a movement after himself. All his noisy radicalization of the collective and his rhetoric added up to a supreme disrespect for the rabble. He represented a simple ruling of a court against him personally as a death sentence on Jonestown, ordering the majority to adopt his frailties and ambitions as their own. In the end, he made his comrades pay with their precious lives for his personal miscalculations in his very personal and very deformed aspirations.

I   Members & Survivors

II Residents & Visitors

III Analysts & Critics

IV Editor & Compiler

V   Appendix & Miscellany ✓

References

(Through out this section the chapter reference at the end of each entry, for example, [Ch. 15] refers to the chapter in this book.)

Print

Cameron, N. (1929). *The Evolution of the Negro.* Georgetown, Guyana: The Argosy Company. [Ch. 15.]

Cummings, L. (1965). *Geography of Guyana.* London, England: Collins. [Ch. 12.]

Cummins, E. (1994). *The Rise and Fall of California's Radical Prison Movement.* Stanford, CA: Stanford University Press. [Ch. 8.]

da Costa, E. V. (1994). *Crowns of Glory, Tears of Blood: The Demerara Slave Rebellion of 1823.* Oxford, England: Oxford University Press. [Ch. 12.]

Granger, D. A. (2005). *National Defence: A Brief History of the Guyana Defence Force 1965 - 2005.* Georgetown, Guyana: Free Press. [Ch. 16.]

Harris, S., & Crittenden, H. (2011). *Father Divine: Holy Husband. Whitefish,* MT: Literary Licensing, LLC. [Ch. 1 & 14.]

Hartman, C., & Carnochan, S. (2002). *City for Sale: The Transformation of San Francisco* (Revised and Updated ed.). Berkeley, CA: UC Press. [Ch. 8.]

Hougan, J. (1999, Summer). *The Secret Life of Jim Jones—A Parapolitical Fuge.* Lobster, (37). [Ch. 14.]

Jagan, C. (1954). *Forbidden Freedom—The Story of British Guiana.* London, U.K.: Lawrence and Wishart. [Ch. 15.]

Jagan, C. (1966). *The West on Trial: My Fight for Guyana's Freedom.* London, U.K.: Michael Joseph. [Ch. 15.]

Jeffries, H. K. (2009). *Bloody Lowndes: Civil Rights and Black Power in Alabama's Black Belt.* New York, NY: NYU Press. [Ch. 8.]

Joseph, P. E. (2006). *Waiting 'Til the Midnight Hour: A History of Black Power in America.* New York, NY: Holt. [Ch. 8.]

Joseph, P. E. (Ed.). (2006). *The Black Power Movement: Rethinking the Civil Rights-Black Power Era.* New York, NY: Routledge. [Ch. 8.]

Josiah, B. P. (2011). *Migration, Mining, and the African Diaspora: Guyana in the Nineteenth and Twentieth Centuries.* New York, NY: Palgrave Macmillan. [Ch. 12.]

Kilduff, M., & Javers, R. (1978). *The Suicide Cult: the Inside Story of the Peoples Temple Sect and the Massacre in Guyana.* New York, NY: Bantam Books. [Ch. 7.]

Kohl, L. J. (2010). *Jonestown Survivor: An Insider's Look.* New York, NY: iUniverse, Inc. [Ch. 1 & 13.]

Levi, K. J. (1981). *Violence and Religious Commitment: Implications of Jim Jones's People's Temple Movement.* University Park, PA: Penn. State Univ. Press. [Ch. 8.]

Lewis, L. (1980). The Jonestown Affair: Towards a Sociological Analysis. *Transition,* 3(1), 421. [Ch. 16.]

Matthews, L. K., & Danns, G. K. (1980). *Communities and Development in Guyana: A Neglected Dimension in Nation Building* [Pamphlet]. Georgetown, Guyana: University of Guyana. [Ch. 7.]

Mills, J. (1979). *Six Years with God: Life Inside Rev. Jim Jones's Peoples Temple.* New York, NY: A&W Publishers. [Ch. 13 & 14.]

Moore, R. (2009). *Understanding Jonestown and Peoples Temple.* Westport, CT: Praegar. [Ch. 14.]

Morrison, A., SJ. (1998). *Justice: The Struggle for Democracy in Guyana, 1952 - 1992.* Georgetown, Guyana: Red Thread. [Ch. 13.]

Payne, G. (1977). *A Rationale for Settlement in Guyana.* Unpublished Paper. [Ch. 7.]

Payne, H. (2001). *10 Days in August, 1834: 10 Days That Changed the World.* Brooklyn, NY: Caribbean Diaspora Press. [Ch. 12.]

People's National Congress. (1974). *Declaration of Sophia* [Pamphlet]. Georgetown, Guyana: People's National Congress. [Ch. 16.]

Peoples Temple. (undated). *Jonestown, A Model of Cooperation* [Pamphlet]. Georgetown, Guyana: Peoples Temple's Agricultural and Medical Project. [Ch. 7 & 16.]

Raleigh, W. (1595). *The Discoverie of Guiana.* London, England: Hakluyt Society. [Ch. 12.]

Reiterman, T., & Jacobs, J. (1982). *Raven: The Untold Story of the Rev. Jim Jones and His People.* New York, NY: Dutton. [Ch. 1, 14, & 18.]

Rodney, W. (2014). *The Groundings with my Brothers.* East Point, GA.: Walter Rodney Press, LLC. [Ch. 9.]

Rodney, W. (1970). *A History of the Upper Guinea Coast 1945 - 1800.* N.Y.C., NY: Monthly Review Press. [Ch. 9.]

Rodney, W. (1972). *How Europe Underdeveloped Africa.* London, U.K.: Bogle-Louverture Publications. [Ch. 9.]

Rodney, W. (1981). *A History of the Guyanese Working People, 1881 - 1905.* Baltimore, MD: John Hopkins University Press. [Ch. 9 & 15.]

Wiesel, E. (2006). *Night.* NY, NY: Hill and Wang (Farrar, Straus, and Giroux). [Ch. 6.]

Working People's Alliance (WPA). *Dayclean.* Georgetown, Guyana. [Newsletter of the Working People's Alliance.] [Ch. 13 & 18.]

Young, A. (1958). *Approaches to Local Self Government in British Guiana.* London, U.K.: Longman and Green. [Ch. 15.]

Electronic

Kohl, L. J. (n.d.). *Sex in the City? Make That, The Commune.* Retrieved July 27, 2014, from Alternative Considerations of Jonestown & Peoples Temple website: http://jonestown.sdsu.edu/?page_id=32698. [Ch. 17.]

Lewis, F. (n.d.). *The Black Panther Party.* Retrieved October 10, 2014, from http://afroamhistory.about.com/od/civil-rightsstruggles/fl/The-Black-Panther-Party.htm. [Ch. 8.]

Mohammed, K. (2003, September 28). *Guyanese Perspectives on Jonestown.* Retrieved July 27, 2014, from Alternative Considerations of Jonestown & Peoples Temple website: http://jonestown.sdsu.edu/?page_id=16579. [Ch. 16.]

Moore, R. (Ed.). (n.d.). http://jonestown.sdsu.edu/. Retrieved July 15, 2014, from Alternative Considerations of Jonestown & Peoples Temple website: http://jonestown.sdsu.edu. [Ch. 18.]

Moore, R. (n.d.). *The Demographics of Jonestown.* Retrieved July 28, 2014, from Alternative Considerations of Jonestown & Peoples Temple website: http://jonestown.sdsu.edu/?page_id=35666. [Ch. 17.]

NewStar.com. News website that carried the efforts of Lela Howard to locate the resting place of her aunt who died in Jonestown. [Ch. 2.]

Film/Video

Pakula, A. J. (Director). (1974). *The Parallax View* [Motion picture]. USA: Paramount. [Ch. 18.]

Nelson, S. (Director). (2006). *Jonestown: The Life and Death of Peoples Temple* (Documentary TV Video). USA: PBS. [Ch. 8 & 18.]

People

Allsopp, Gertrude — market woman and PNC stalwart of Georgetown. [Ch. 17.]

Amos, Sharon — the equivalent of a public relations officer for Jonestown. She was stationed at the Georgetown Lamaha Gardens office. In unison with the mass suicide/murder event in Jonestown, she killed her small children and herself in that offsite location. [Ch. 3.]

Andrews, Desmond — a medical auxiliary in the employ of the government of Guyana and stationed in the Northwest District at the time of the tragedy. His story is told in Chapter 3. [Ch. 3.]

Annibourne, Neville — veteran local journalist who accompanied the U.S. delegation to Jonestown as a representative of the government of Guyana. He survived the massacre. [Ch. 3.]

Ayinde — communications specialist whose business was to follow affairs of state very closely. His story is told in Chapter 3. [Ch. 3.]

Barker, Lloyd — Commissioner of Police at the time of the Jonestown tragedy. Held the position from 1977 to 1985, which were turbulent years in Guyana. Died July 20, 1999, age 68. [Ch. 9.]

Barnes, Emma — strong-willed woman of Buxton, East Coast Demerara. [Ch. 17.]

Barnwell, Kenneth — Registrar of the Supreme Court of Guyana at the time of the Stoen custody matter that involved Jim Jones. Died October 5, 2013, age 85. [Ch. 9.]

Bear, Teddy (real name is Chris Lewis) — big, black, strong and imposing figure of a man. Served as enforcer in the Temple. His violent death on the streets in America is believed to have been orchestrated by Jim Jones, who related the death to his congregation as fulfillment of his (Jones's) prophecy: bad things happen to you if you leave the Temple. [Ch. 1.]

Beck, Don — a former teacher who became a Temple member. He copied and sorted the diary kept by Edith Roller. (See entry under her name). [Ch. 1 & 18.]

Becton, George Wilson—messianic reverend of Harlem prior to the Peace Movement. Father Divine is seen by some as filling the void after his death. [Ch. 14.]

Bishop, Aubrey—became Chief Justice in 1992 and Chancellor of the Judiciary in 1985. As one of the Justices of the Supreme Court of Guyana, he is remembered for the principled stand he took in exiting from the Stoen child custody case involving the Rev. Jim Jones. Died in 2013, age 81. [Ch. 9 & 14.]

Blanco, Kathleen—Governor of Louisiana, who, on request, intervened to locate the grave of Peoples Temple victim, Mary Pearl Willis. [Ch. 2.]

Bollers, Sir Harold—Chief Justice (1966 to 1980) during the Jonestown times and the generally turbulent years in Guyana's history. Died in 2006, age 91. [Ch. 9 & 14.]

Bourne, Caroline—strong Garveyite of Kitty. Was prominent in protesting the 1948 shooting of Indian sugar workers of Enmore, East Coast Demerara. [Ch. 17.]

Burgan, Rev Canon W. G.—this priest is on record as calling the martyrdom of Rev. John Smith "a mere fluke." [Ch. 12.]

Burnham, Forbes

Carmichael, Stokeley—born in Trinidad; became a strident black-American activist during the Black Power movement in the USA. [Ch. 6.]

Carter, Rosalynn—wife of U.S. President Jimmy Carter. The Peoples Temple used her name (and photograph) to endorse their mission. [Ch. 11.]

Clarke, John Henrik—well-known scholar of African history. He also wrote incisively on Father Divine and his movement. [Ch. 14.]

Culley, Nana—matriarch of Buxton, East Coast Demerara. She locked the door of the village office preventing a village overseer from gaining entry. [Ch. 17.]

Damon—freed as a slave by the Abolition of Slavery Act of 1833 but forced to work for the former master for six more years, this ex-slave staged a passive protest. He was tried and sentenced to death by hanging. [Ch. 12.]

Davis, Angela—internationally known African-American activist during the Black Power era in the USA. Her name was also cited as a reference for the Peoples Temple. [Ch. 11.]

Divine, Father—(Father Major Jealous Divine), prominent African-American religious leader of the 1930s. He founded the Peace Mission, originally dismissed as a cult, but now seen as a precursor of the Civil Rights Movement. [Ch. 1 & 14.]

Divine, Mother—wife of Father Divine. See 'Father Divine.' [Ch. 14.]

Dodd, David—expatriate sociologist and scholar in criminology; worked at the University of Guyana during the Jonestown years. [Ch. 14.]

Evans, Sir Godfrey—town planner and land settlement expert. Recommended Makouria in the Northwest District as the ideal site for the capital city because of its high ground. He also gave details for the proposed settlement and transportation network. [Ch. 5.]

Feodor Timofeyev—Acting Ambassador and Chief of the Press Department of the USSR Embassy in Guyana; visited Jonestown as guest of Jim Jones and was very complimentary in his remarks. [Ch. 18.]

Field-Ridley, Shirley—the Minister of Information at the time of Jonestown. A London-trained lawyer, she was a leading activist both at home and in the Caribbean. Was married to Hamilton Greene. Died in June, 1982, age 45, having retired from active politics a few years before. [Ch. 11.]

Fortson, Hue—Jonestown survivor. His wife and son died in Jonestown. He was a close aide to the Rev. Jim Jones and held the position of Associate Pastor of the Peoples Temple in Los Angeles. He was in San Francisco working on Temple matters on the day of the tragedy, November 18, 1978. He continues his religious work in the U.S. His story is told in Chapter 1 of this book. [Ch. 1.]

Fortson, Hue Ishi—son of Hue Fortson. He perished in Jonestown. Hue Fortson's story is told in Chapter 1 of this book. [Ch. 1.]

Fortson, Rhonda—wife of Hue Fortson. She perished in Jonestown. Hue Fortson's story is told in Chapter 1 of this book. [Ch. 1.]

People

Gang of Eight—a group of Temple members in San Francisco who protested in writing the excesses, especially sexual, practiced in the organization. [Ch. 18.]

Gaskin, Winifred—government minister in the administration of Forbes Burnham. [Ch. 16.]

Gladstone, Jack—deacon of the church and one of the leaders of the 1823 uprising. [Ch. 12.]

Granger, David A.—currently Leader of the Opposition in Guyana's Parliament. He retired from military service with the rank of Brigadier in 1994 after serving as National Security Adviser to President Hoyte, and as Commander of the Guyana Defence Force (1979-90). **Update**: Granger's alliance won the elections of May 11, 2015, and he became the president of Guyana. [Ch. 16.]

Greene, Hamilton—senior minister of government, who spearheaded the cooperatives at Port Kaituma, among many other projects. [Ch. 5.]

Hargrave, Neva Sly—Jonestown survivor. Her story is told in Chapter 1 of this book. [Ch. 1.]

Harris, Herbert—resident of Monroe, Louisiana, who helped locate the burial place of Peoples Temple victim, Mary Pearl Willis. [Ch. 2.]

Harris, Sara—a former member of the Peace Mission, she has written firsthand about the class and race structure of the organization. See 'Harris S. & Crittenden H.' in the *References* page under *Print*. [Ch. 1.]

Hill, David—see Rabi Washington in this listing. [Ch. 6.]

Hoogenheim, Van—Dutch Governor at the time of the Berbice Slave Rebellion of 1763. [Ch. 12.]

Howard, Lela—niece of Peoples Temple victim Mary Pearl Willis. Lela tells her aunt's story to the editor of this book, which appears in Chapter 2. [Ch. 2.]

Ijames, Archie—faithful and long standing Peoples Temple member. He told Jim Jones that the organization was a travesty. Jim Jones wanted to have him killed. See details, as related by Hue Fortson, in Chapter 1. (Archie Ijames died May 30, 1993.) [Ch. 1.]

Jacobs, Neville — see Koama, Ohene in this listing. [Ch. 15.]

Jitu Weusi — African American attending the 1970 Seminar of Pan Africanist and Black Revolutionary Activists in Georgetown, Guyana. He is remembered for posing a question to Prime Minister Burnham, who responded that the same sanctuary offered to freedom fighters from Africa would be offered to African Americans. [Ch. 18.]

Jones, Kenneth — A resident in the Jonestown neighborhood. His story is told in Chapter 3. [Ch. 3.]

Jones, Marceline — wife of Jim Jones. She also perished in the tragedy. [Ch. 3.]

Jones, Stephan — son of Jim Jones. He survived the tragedy. [Ch. 1.]

Khan, Rafiq — General Manager of the Radio Demerara radio station and Lecturer at the University of Guyana. He is considered without equal in broadcasting in Guyana. Died October, 2014, age 82. [Ch. 3.]

Koama, Ohene — formerly Neville Jacobs. Co-founder of the Young Farmers' Cooperative. Ohene was killed in Georgetown in 1979. His death is generally believed to be a case of murder by the Death Squad . [Ch. 15.]

Kohl, Laura Johnston — Jonestown survivor. Her story is told in Chapter 1 of this book. She has also written about the Peoples Temple (Kohl, 2010) and continues to serve as a person with first-hand knowledge of the functioning of the Peoples Temple. [Ch. 1.]

Lewis, Chris — see Bear, Teddy in this listing. [Ch. 1.]

Lillowattie — a known fatality of pseudo African magic, which practice was legally classified as obeah. [Ch. 6.]

McLean, Norman — (Brigadier General) was head of the Guyana Defence Force during turbulent political times that included the death of Walter Rodney. He retired in 1990. Just before assuming the top position in the GDF, he was head of the para-military Guyana National Service (GNS). [Ch. 16.]

Mayfield, Julian — Black-American activist and film star who became a close adviser to Prime Minister Forbes Burnham. [Ch. 6.]

Miller, Christine—rank and file African-American Temple member who perished in the fiasco. Though not a member of the inner circle, she enjoyed special privileges primarily because she was not a down-and-out recruit but had her own home, car, etc. that she relinquished to help the mission. She stood up to Jim Jones and advised against the suicide but was over powered. [Ch. 17.]

Mohamed, Khaleel—Guyanese-born professor of Religion at San Diego State University (SDSU) and a core faculty member of SDSU's Center for Islamic and Arabic Studies. [Ch. 13.]

Mohamed, Wazir—Assistant Professor, Sociology, at Indiana University. Done scholarly work on the forgotten role of African Guyanese farmers in the rice sector. [Ch. 15.]

Moore, Rebecca—professor in the Department of Religious Studies at San Diego State University and manager of the Website "Alternative Considerations of Jonestown and Peoples Temple." Also, author of several books and papers. [Ch. 18.]

Mootoo, Leslie—well-known medical doctor. Visited Jonestown. [Ch. 3.]

Morrison, Andrew—Jesuit priest and civil rights activist, who authored the seminal work *Justice: The Struggle for Democracy in Guyana, 1952 – 1992*. [Ch. 13.]

Nkrumah, Kwame—first prime minister of independent Ghana. Later overthrown and exiled. [Ch. 6.]

Prokes, Mike—a television newsman before he joined the Temple to become its chief press contact. He inadvertently escaped the tragedy because he was assigned to carry a suitcase of cash to the Soviet Embassy in Georgetown. Less than four months after the disaster, he took his own life. [Ch. 18.]

Quamina—a former slave who became a deacon of the church and one of the leaders of the 1823 uprising. [Ch. 12.]

Rabbi Washington—an African American, (David Hill is his real name). came to Guyana after skipping bail in Cleveland, Ohio, USA. He set up a cult-like group called the House of Israel. It functioned as an enforcer and street thug for the ruling political party (PNC). [Ch. 1 & 13.]

Reid, Ptolemy—deputy prime minister in Burnham's administration. [Ch. 16.]

Ritterman, Tim—co-author of one of the most incisive books on Jonestown. It is titled *Raven: The Untold Story of the Rev. Jim Jones and his People*. See 'Ritterman, T. & Jacobs, J.' in the *References* page under *Print*. [Ch. 1.]

Roller Edith—Known for the diaries and journals she kept of daily life in Jonestown. She was a member of the Temple from its earliest days. Her writings reflect the quiet and simple life of the ordinary folks in the commune, and includes entries of suicide practices and talks of moving to Cuba or Russia. She is said to have been an ex-CIA person. She too perished in the disaster. [Ch. 18.]

Sanders, Suzanne Shukuru Copeland—U.S. citizen who worked as a Nurse/Midwife in Guyana. [Ch. 3.]

Scott, Keith—comes from a family well-grounded in the political and cultural development of Guyana. He continues that family tradition and is currently a minister of the Guyana Government as part of APNU. His story is told in Chapter 3. [Ch. 3 & 16.]

Sharma, Rohan—pilot in the employ of the Guyana Defence Force (GDF). Occasionally flew from Ogle airstrip outside of Georgetown to the Northwest (Jonestown). [Ch. 3.]

Shultz, Molly—a known fatality of pseudo Hindi magic, which practice was legally classified as obeah. [Ch. 6.]

Singh, Dr. Balwant—practicing medical doctor in Guyana and visitor to Jonestown. [Ch. 3.]

Smith, Rev. John—the officiating priest at Bethel Chapel at Le Resouvenir. He rendered assistance to the slaves in the 1823 uprising, was charged for treason, found guilty, and died in prison while awaiting sentence. He is considered a martyr in Guyanese history. [Ch. 12.]

Stoen, John—a six-year-old over whom a custody case brought by his parents against Rev. Jim Jones was opened in the Guyana courts. No ruling was made in the matter, and the child perished in the Jonestown tragedy. [Ch. 9.]

Synanon—a drug-rehabilitation organization in the San Francisco area that became a powerhouse in its own right. It provided supplies to Peoples Temple and functioned as a conduit for goods from other donors. [Ch. 1.]

Van Sertima, Laurence—a professional snake handler and visitor to Jonestown. [Ch. 3.]

Willis, Mary Pearl—Temple member who perished in the November 18, 1978, tragedy. Her story is told by her niece Lela Howard, who has established a foundation in her memory. See Chapter 2 for her story. [Ch. 2.]

Wilson, Roy—master cooperative farmer and member of the 'Wilson' family lineage associated with pioneering agricultural work. [Ch. 15.]

Wright, Annie—resident of Campbellville, Georgetown, and a pioneer in the Jaganite PPP movement. Later went over to the PNC. [Ch. 17.]

Young, Alan—author of the pioneering work Approaches to Local Self Government in British Guiana. Was General Manager of the Transport and Harbor Department, and affectionately regarded as the first academic village historian of British Guiana. [Ch. 15.]

Places

[Most of the names are for places in the Northwest District of Guyana, where Peoples Temple was based. A lot of the names are Aboriginal is origin, reflective of the original inhabitants of the region. A few words are also of French and Dutch origin as those two nations preceded the British in colonizing Guyana. — E.K.]

Ankoko Island — formerly part of the territory of Guyana but was taken over by Venezuela in the border dispute the two countries have.

Arakaka — gold-mining town in the NWD, about 12 miles southerly of Port Kaituma.

Barima — part of the administrative region of Barima/Waini in the NWD.

Berbice — one of the 3 counties in Guyana.

Beterverwagting—village on the East Coast of Demerara.

Bottom Floor — the entertainment center in NWD.

Butenabu — location in the Mahaicony River Basin, ECD.

Buxton — historic village purchased by Africans following emancipation from slavery (1838).

Campbellville —thriving community of greater Georgetown, the capital.

Catherine — not well known village on the East Coast of Demerara.

Clemwood —community up the Demerara River in the Essequibo region.

Demerara — one of the three counties in Guyana.

Dora — farming community off the Linden/Soesdyke Highway.

East Coast — short form for East Coast Demerara.

A New Look at J O N E S T O W N

Eldorado — the fabled golden city in the Guianas, which brought European explorers and treasure hunters.

Enmore — village on the East Coast of Demerara, known for the five strikers (Enmore Martyrs) killed in 1948.

Essequibo — one of three counties in Guyana.

Georgetown — the capital city and seat of government in Guyana.

British Guiana — (Guiana, for short) the pre-independence name of the country.

'Heavens' — residence in the hotels owned and/or operated by the Peace Mission in the USA.

Kaituma — short name for Port Kaituma.

Kitty — thriving community of greater Georgetown, the capital.

Kumaka — remote community in the Barima/Waini region.

Kuru Kururu — the first and largest village on the Soesdyke/Linden Highway.

La Belle Alliance — sparsely inhabited village on the Essequibo Coast.

Lamaha Gardens — a residential suburb in the city of Georgetown. In this area, the Temple occupied a site that was considered the Georgetown office of Jonestown and served also as living quarters for the members stationed there. Members visiting Georgetown from the Northwest District would stay there as well.

Le Ressouvenir — estate on the East Coast of Demerara.

Linden — the new name for the Mackenzie/Wismar area, taken from the first name of Prime Minister Linden Forbes Sampson Burnham.

Long Creek — small settlement up the Soesdyke/Linden Highway.

Lourdes — in France; major place for Roman Catholic pilgrimages because of the reported appearances of the Blessed Virgin Mary and occurrence of miraculous healings.

Mabaruma — administrative center for Barima/Waini region in the NWD.

Mackenzie — the bauxite mining town that, along with neighboring Wismar, was renamed Linden, the first name of Prime Minister Burnham.

Mahaicony (River) — small river that drains into the Atlantic Ocean. The village of Mahaicony is at the mouth of the river.

Makouria — was recommended as the place to relocate the capitol because of the high ground and the entrances available. Sir Godfrey Evans made this recommendation in his writings on the resettlement of Guiana.

Marudi — mining area in the deep southern region of Guyana.

Matthews Ridge — small town in the Barima/Waini region in the NWD.

Melanie Damishana — a planned community that served as the model of government sponsored and approved development. "Melanie" is the name of one of Mr. Burnham's daughters, and "Damishana" is an Amerindian word meaning village.

Moblissa — also known as Moblissa River and Moblissa Creek, small community along the Linden/Soesdyke Highway.

Moco-Moco — unspoilt area in the Rupunini region just a short distance from Lethem.

Mon Repos — well-known village on the East Coast of Demerara.

Mora Passage — a tidal creek located in the Barima/Waini region.

Morawhanna — settlement on the left bank of the Barima River in the Barima/Waini region.

New River — river that runs through South America (including Suriname and Guyana). The border dispute between the two countries is known as the New River Triangle.

Northwest District — (preferred form in this book, but referred to outside of this book as: NWD, Northwest, and North West District).

Places

Ogle — village on the East Coast of Demerara

Parika — thriving township port on the East Bank of the Essequibo River

Port Kaituma — settlement in the NWD originally developed to facilitate manganese extraction

Port Mourant — established village in Berbice, the birthplace of Cheddi Jagan

Moruca — this Amerindian village is located in the NWD

NWD — abbreviation for Northwest District

Soesdyke — located near the Cheddi Jagan International Airport, it is here when the Soesdyke/Linden Highway begins

Timehri — location and name of Guyana's international airport, Cheddie Jagan International Airport, Timehri.

Wanaima — community in the Barima/Waini region, NWD.

Yarakita — small community along the Soesdyke/Linden Highway that was designated for sand mining.

Yarowkabra — community in the Barima/Waini region, NWD.

Waini — short name for Barima/Waini.

Wismar — town next door to the bauxite city of Mackenzie, that together were renamed Linden.

Organizations

AAA — Afro-American Association. Created out of the fervent of the 1960s and based in the Berkeley/Oakland district of the San Francisco Bay Area, it promoted black pride and achievement. Many of the black leaders that later arose were inspired by the teachings of this group. [Ch. 8.]

African Manganese Company — The company that mined the manganese ore in the Northwest District from 1960 to 1969. [Ch. 12.]

ASCRIA — African Society for Cultural Relations with Independent Africa. A cultural organization formed by Eusi Kwayana to address and promote ties between black Guyanese and other black peoples outside of Guyana. [Ch. 2, 3, 15, & 18.]

Bethel Chapel — Church of the Rev. John Smith, who was sympathetic to the cause of the slave rebels. [Ch. 12.]

Black Panther Party — Beginning in around the mid-1960s, it became the most militant black organization of the era. It contrasted sharply with Martin Luther King's non-violent movement. [Ch. 8.]

BSU — Black Student Union. Formed around UC Berkley and San Francisco State University and later picked up followers in high schools. This movement is credited with placing black studies on the academic curriculum. [Ch. 8.]

COINTELPRO — (COunter INTELigence PROgram). Established by the FBI and equipped with more sophisticated programs for infiltrating and neutralizing militant groups. [Ch. 8 & 18.]

Cuffy Farmers' Cooperative Society — A cooperative sponsored and supported by the Guyana Government. [Ch. 7.]

Disciples of Christ — The church Jim Jones was previously associated with as a pastor before he formed Peoples Temple. [Ch. 14.]

DWIC — Dutch West India Company. Chartered by the Dutch government to administer and exploit territories under Dutch control. [Ch. 12.]

East Uhuru School of New York — Black nationalist group which taught nation-building skills to its members. Also had an independent school called Uhuru Sasa. [Ch. 1 & 3.]

GAC — Guyana Airways Corporation, the government-owned and operated airline. [Ch.11.]

GDF — Guyana Defence Force. The national army of the state. [Ch.13.]

GNS — Guyana National Service. A paramilitary body that focused on nation building while developing the 'cadres' for developing the interior of the country. [Ch. 13.]

GPF — Guyana Police Force. The law enforcement agency of the state. [Ch. 13.]

GPM — Guyana Peoples Militia. A paramilitary organization whose creation was prompted by the border dispute with Venezuela. Its members were to continue their usual lives but be prepared to defend the country. [Ch. 13.]

House of Israel — This controversial body was formed by a fugitive U.S. citizen. It appeared as a church but had close ties with the ruling political party. There is now documentary evidence that it was also a street enforcer for that party. [Ch. 13.]

HUAC — House Un-American Activities Committee. Investigative committee of the U.S. House of Representatives. Created in 1938 to identify citizens with Nazi ties but later expanded its function to include those suspected of other subversive and disloyal behavior. [Ch. 8.]

Key West — Government cooperative operating in the Northwest District. [Ch. 5.]

London Missionary Society — The religious body that established churches in the colonies and appointed presiding priests. [Ch. 12.]

Marudi Cooperative — This coop in the Mahaicony River Basin was unique in that it included hands-on field workers as well as technically trained personnel. Lennox Massay was one of the scientific-minded persons in the group. [Ch. 15.]

NGS — National Guard Service. Created specifically to protect government personnel and state property from theft and subversive activity. [Ch. 13.]

Peace Mission — The movement founded by Father Divine. See 'Father Divine' in this section under 'People.' [Ch. 1 & 14.]

Peoples Militia — A volunteer paramilitary force that was intended to supplement the official forces in event of need. 'Every citizen a soldier' was its credo. [Ch. 13.]

PNC — People's National Congress, the political party in office at the time, which was headed by L.F.S. Burnham, the founder-leader. [Ch. 1, 6, 7, 13, & 16.]

PPP — People's Progressive Party, the main political opposition party in Guyana at that time, which was headed by Cheddi Jagan, its chief founder. [Ch. 1, 13, 16, 17, & 18.]

Ptolemy Reid Rehabilitation Center — Health facility named after the deputy prime minister of Guyana. [Ch.16.]

Public Hospital Georgetown (PHG) — This is the main government hospital and it is located in the capital city of Georgetown. It has since been renamed Georgetown Public Hospital Corporation (GPHC). [Ch. 3.]

R.C. Sacred Heart Church — The Roman Catholic Sacred Heart Church on Main Street, Georgetown. It is here that Jim Jones and the Peoples Temple made their public appearance in Guyana with a healing service. The R.C. officials subsequently explained that they allowed the church to be used as a goodwill gesture, not knowing "miracles" were going to be performed. [Ch. 16.]

Radio Demerara — One of two radio broadcasting stations in Guyana at the time. [Ch. 3.]

Synanon — A drug-rehabilitation organization in San Francisco that became a powerhouse in its own right. It generously donated to the Peoples Temple. [Ch. 1.]

The Jonestown Institute — This is the unit in the Department of Religious Studies at San Diego State University that sponsors the website "Alternative Considerations of Jonestown and Peoples Temple," (Moore, n.d.). [Ch. 1.]

The Mary Pearl Willis Foundation — Foundation created to honor the memory of Peoples Temple victim Mary Pearl Willis. [The foundation and website appear to be defunct at time of publication of this book.] [Ch. 2.]

Timehri Airport — The international airport of Guyana, now renamed the Cheddi Jagan International Airport. [Ch. 13.]

University of Guyana — The only tertiary degree-granting institution in Guyana at the time. [Ch. 3.]

West Bank — Government cooperative operating in the Northwest District. [Ch. 5.]

WPA — Working Peoples Alliance, the political party associated with the late Dr. Walter Rodney. [Ch. 13.]

WRSM — Women's Revolutionary Socialist Movement, the women's arm of the ruling PNC political party. [Ch. 13.]

Young Farmer's Cooperative — This was another very productive agricultural coop. Its founders were Roy Wilson of the well-known Wilson family and Neville Jacobs (later Ohene Koama). [Ch. 15.]

YSM (Young Socialist Movement) — Youth arm of the then ruling Peoples National Congress political party. [Ch. 18.]

Miscellaneous Terms

Aapan jaat — from Hindu, and translates to "your own kind." First used in Guyana during national elections in the form "vote aapan jaat." [Ch. 18.]

Abattoir — The common expression in Guyana for a slaughter house.

Toshaos — Head or chief of the Amerindian community in Guyana, 1952 – 1992. [Ch. 13.]

'Came from above' — an expression developed in Guyana to refer to the topmost level of authority. The term is generally cited to reinforce that an obviously outrageous directive or request had its authorship from the highest level possible. [Ch. 6.]

Comrade (Cde. for short) — a new mode of address that was promulgated by the government of the day to replace the traditional Mr., Mrs., Sir, Madam, etc. Its introduction was thought to be in keeping with the egalitarian goals of socialism. It caused more confusion than anything and seems to have naturally faded away. [Ch. 4.]

Drugstore — the local word for pharmacy. [Ch. 3.]

Fair weather – adjective used to describe something that only works or functions in the dry season. For example, 'fair weather road,' means that when the rains come the road will be washed away. [Ch. 4 & 6.]

Hippie — expression used to describe the participants of the counter culture movement that developed in the Haight-Ashbury district of San Francisco and spread across the U.S. in the 1960s. It was noted for its liberal outlook on drugs, sex, race, politics, etc. [Ch. 8.]

Itabo — means "another way." It describes that part of a river that branches off and rejoins the mother by another route, probably evading a huge obstacle like a rock. [Ch. 10.]

Jaadu – the Indian counterpart of 'obeah.' See 'obeah' below. [Ch. 6.]

Manaharva — a forgotten hero of the indigenous people who conducted high level diplomacy with foreign rulers. [Ch. 10.]

Mission Field — refers to the territories and the local peoples who were identified to be Christianized by foreign religious missionaries. [Ch. 18.]

Obeah — an unofficial African religious practice. The Indian counterpart of this practice was called 'jaadu.' See 'jaadu' above. [Ch. 6.]

Riverain — this is the Guyanese version of the standard English word 'riverine.' [Ch. 15.]

Tailhook — refers to the allegations of mass sexual assault by the U.S. military at the 35the Annual Tailhook Association Symposium in 1991 in Las Vegas, Nevada. [Ch. 17.]

Ombudsman – a judicial appointee to whom charges against public officials may be made, and who must investigate impartially. [Ch. 09.]

White Night — code name for the mass suicide. This code was used in preparation and rehearsal for the November 18, 1978 fiasco. [Ch. 3.]

Map of Guyana

Area referred to as the
Northwest District (NWD)

Courtesy of Klaus Kästle of Nations Online Project (12-3-15)

Other Works by Kwayana

"Kwayana's collected writings ... will astonish the world."
— *Dr. Rupert Roopnaraine*

[Kwayana's multi-faceted writings defy classification and go back as far as the 1940s. The sampling here is taken prematurely from Dr. Nigel Westmaas's work in progress. — P.D.S., Publisher]

Plays & Opera

Prodigal Daughter. (1946). Georgetown, Guyana: Diocesan Youth Movement. [First play].

Christus the Messiah. (1950s). Georgetown, Guyana. [Opera with chorus: lyrics by Kwayana; music by Cecilene Baird].

Wayside Preacher. (1950s). Georgetown, Guyana.

Promised Land. (1965). Georgetown, Guyana. [Won 'Best Play Produced,' 'Best Junior Actor', and 'Best Junior Group' awards].

Rookmin Mai & Auntie Pet. (1970s). Georgetown, Guyana. [Street play performed at roadsides].

Queen of the Riot. (1981). Georgetown, Guyana.

King on Trial. (1981). Georgetown, Guyana.

Lyrics

Song of the Demerara Youth Rally. (1950s). Georgetown, Guyana.

Oh, Fighting Men. (1952). Lyrics for song of the People's Progressive Party (PPP).

The Battle Song. (1958). Lyrics for song of the People's National Congress (PNC).

People's Power. (1982). Lyrics for song of the Working People's Alliance (WPA).

Books, Booklets, Essays

The Boiling Pot: What's in It? (2013). Birmingham, U.K.: The Guyana Examiner. Vol 1, No. 2, (June, 2013). [Long essay].

Walter Rodney: His Last Days and Campaigns. (2010). Birmingham, U.K.: R. Ferdinand-Lalljie Publishers.

The Morning After. (2005). Georgetown, Guyana: Guyana-Caribbean Politics.

Scars of Bondage: A First Study of the Slave Colonial Experience of Africans in Guyana. (2002). [Co-author, Tchaiko Kwayana]. Georgetown, Guyana: Free Press.

Guyana: No Guilty Race. (1998). Georgetown, Guyana: Free Press.

Buxton-Friendship in Print and Memory. (1999). Georgetown, Guyana: Red Thread Press.

Paul Robeson: Constant Star. (1998). Georgetown, Guyana: WPA. [Booklet].

Gang Gang: Thirty African Proverbs. (1997). Georgetown, Guyana: Red Thread Press. [Kindle edition published (2014). Birmingham, U.K.: R. Ferdinand-Lalljie Publishers.]

Groovy Grammar. (1996). Georgetown, Guyana: Red Thread Press.

Footnotes to the "West on Trial." (1988). Commentary on Cheddi Jagan's classic work. [Long essay].

More than Survival: The Afro-Guyanese and the Nations. (1988). Paper presented at the Genesis of a Nation Conference sponsored by the University of Guyana & the Guyana Commemoration Commission at the Pegasus Hotel, Georgetown, Guyana.

More than Survival: A View of the Indo-Guyanese Contribution to Social Change. (1988). Paper presented at the Genesis of a Nation Conference sponsored by the University of Guyana & the Guyana Commemoration Commission at the Pegasus Hotel, Georgetown, Guyana.

Race in the Guyana Revolution. (1987). [Long essay].

The Poetry of Martin Carter. (1986). [Long essay].

Walter Rodney. (1985). [Booklet].

Politics of the Heart. (1984). Havana, Cuba: Anales del Caribe, No. 4/5, 1984/5. [Republished 2000 in Stewart Brown's (Editor) "All Are Involved: The Art of Martin Carter." Leeds: Peepal Tree Press].

Walter Rodney Lives: An Analysis of Walter Rodney's Contribution to National and International Struggle for Bread and Justice. (1981). London, England: Sign of the Times (periodical).

Racial Insecurity and the Old Politics. (1975). [Long essay].

On Pseudo-Socialism and the PNC. (1973). [Long essay].

Teachings of the Cultural Revolution. (1968). Georgetown, Guyana: ASCRIA.

Next Witness: An Appeal to World Opinion. (1962). Georgetown, Guyana: Labour Advocate. [Republished 1999 with a new introduction by the author].

Preface, Foreword, Afterword

Afterword. (2006). Tim Hector, Humanist—Political Values, and National Reconstruction. "Tim Hector: A Caribbean Radical's Story" by Paul Buhle. Jackson: University Press of Mississippi.

Preface. (1985). "Rasta and Resistance: From Garvey to Rodney" by Horace Campbell. Trenton, New Jersey: Africa World Press.

Foreword. (1954). "Poems of Resistance from British Guiana" by Martin Carter. [Republished 2000 in Stewart Brown's (Editor) "All Are Involved: The Art of Martin Carter." Leeds: Peepal Tree Press].

Preface. (1953). Martin Carter's "Poems of Resistance." Georgetown, Guyana.

Foreword. (1952). "Fight for Freedom: Waddington Constitution Exposed" by Cheddi Jagan. Georgetown, Guyana.

Book Review

Review. (2010). "Guyana Wanderer." [Short story by Jan Carew]. GuyaneseOnline. WordPress.com. July 2010 issue.

Review. (2006). "Primacy of the Eye" by Rupert Roopnaraine. GuyanaCaribbeanPolitics.com. July 21, 2006.

Review. (2003). "Reclaiming Zimbabwe: The Exhaustion of the Patriarchal Mode of Liberation" by Horace Campbell.

Review. (2003). "Giving Voice to the Poor: Poverty Alleviation in West Bengal and Bangladesh" by Ruhul Amin & Maurice St. Pierre.

Review. (2002). "Contributions towards the Resolution of Conflict in Guyana" by Judaman Seecoomar.

Review. (2002). "Ten Days that Shook the World" by Tommy Payne.] Georgetown, Guyana: Guyana Review, May 2002.

Review. (1998). "Themes in African-Guyanese History" by Winston McGowan, James Rose, and David Granger (Editors). Georgetown, Guyana: Emancipation 1999-2000.

Review. (1993). "Jaguar and the Flute" by Churamanie Bissundyal. Georgetown, Guyana: Stabroek News, July 11, 1993.

Review. (1984). "Thirty Years a Civil Servant," by A.J. Seymour. Georgetown, Guyana: Kyk-Over-Al, No. 30, Dec 1984.

Review. (1964). "Consciencism," by Kwame Nkrumah. Accra, Ghana: Spark.

Film Review

The Film as History and a Work of Art. (1979). Review of "Terror and the Time" by the Victor Jara Collective.

Blessed the Land of Many Mantras. (1987). Review of "Maha Shiva Ratri: an Experience in Belief."

About the Author

Eusi Kwayana, formerly Sydney King (born April 4, 1925), is a Guyanese thinker and cultural activist, educator, dramatist, and writer. A founder member of the Peoples Progressive Party (PPP) in 1950, he became a minister in the PPP government of 1953. To this day, his actions have been inextricably bound up with political development of Guyana, spanning the colonial struggle for nationhood through post-independence rule.

In 1957 he became a senior member of the newly formed Peoples National Congress (PNC) from which he was expelled in 1961 for having views divergent from the party hierarchy's. Nevertheless, Kwayana continued to support the PNC. In 1964, with help from others, he founded ASCRIA (African Society for Cultural Relations with Independent Africa), a Pan-Africanist cultural organization.

He parted company with the PNC in 1974 and helped found the Working People's Alliance (WPA), serving as its Member of Parliament in 1985. He is remembered, among other dramatic acts, for his a one-man public fast for the restoration of democracy and end of corruption.

Kwayana is the author of 10 previous books, including *Scars of Bondage* and (with Tchaiko Kwayana) *Walter Rodney: His Last Days and Campaigns.* He also wrote the lyrics of the party songs of Guyana's three leading political parties, the PPP, PNC and WPA.